P9-CQK-538

CATHOLICS
IN ENGLISH CANADA

A popular history

Volume I: 1790-1900

Kintore College
75 Charles St W
Toronto, ON
Canada
416-944-8323

MURRAY NICOLSON

Copyright © 2000

Author

Murray William Nicolson earned a B.A. (Hons. History) at St. Jerome's College and an M.A. at the University of Waterloo where he was awarded the Arts Graduate Fellowship. He completed his PhD at the University of Guelph in 1981. His thesis is entitled "The Catholic Church and the Irish in Victorian Toronto." Subsequently he did extensive research on social history of Ontario with regards to Catholicism and has published many articles on the subject. He taught history for a number of years at Wilfrid Laurier University. He is now retired and resides in Newmarket, Ontario.

Publication data
ISBN 1-895599-07-6
Information from Cataloguing:
Canadian Cataloguing in Publication Data
Nicolson, Murray W. (Murray William)
Catholics in English Canada: a popular history
Contents: v. 1. 1790-1900.
Includes index.
ISBN 1-895599-09-1(v.1)
1. Catholic Church — Canada— History. 2. Catholics — Canada — History. I. Life Ethics Centre. II. Title.
BX 1421. 2. N52

Printer:
Ave Maria Press, Toronto, ON
Cover design:
Ryan Hryciuk

Catholic Insight is a publication of Life Ethics Information Centre, a non-profit company. Those wishing to support the Centre may make a tax-deductable donation to:

The Society for Catholic Life and Culture
813 Hillcrest Road Pickering, ON L1W 2P5

1st Printing, June 2000: 1-3,000

PUBLISHER

Life Ethics Information Centre
104 Bond Street, Suite 304
Toronto, ON M5B 1X9
Tel (416) 204-9601   Fax (416) 204-1027
e-mail:catholic@catholicinsight.com

Contents

FOREWORD

History is concerned with the unique, that is with the events that shape and form either a single person or a particular group of people. Therefore, we have family histories, or a history of people living in a particular town or city, or a history of this or that ethnic group or perhaps of a province. Finally, we have histories of nations.

In each of these histories one must find the bond that ties a group together, and often—as is the case above—these bonds are not mutually exclusive: a family lives in a city, in a province, which, in turn, is part of a nation. Other histories also fit this pattern, such as that of a business, or a union, or a railroad. Beyond that, there are histories of even larger themes, such as the histories of warfare, philosophy, theology, and education.

Perhaps the strongest bond of all among people, next to that of blood, is religion. It certainly reaches beyond state boundaries, or languages, or ethnicity, though in the writing of a history it is often necessary to join with one or two of these other aspects. This is the case with our volume here: its scope is restricted to English-speaking Catholics in Canada.

The bond among Catholics is obviously their faith. This in turn finds its institutional expression in parishes and dioceses united to the Holy See in Rome. The faith itself is a participation in the life of Jesus Christ, who founded His Church 2000 years ago. Not only do Catholics seek to imitate the Lord Jesus but, through the sacramental system, they participate in the life of Christ Himself who is at once human and divine. Therefore the literature, theology, philosophy and, at times, even the politics, of the universal Church from the time of Christ onwards remain of the utmost importance to the "local" Church in Canada. Because Christ brought eternal life and entrusted His Church with this "Gospel" of Good News, the Catholic faith places the eternal above the temporal, with the former judging the latter. Catholics recognize that the temporal order has its own jurisdiction and authority, but they also believe that this order is not independent; it must be exercised in harmony with the eternal good.

The principle that there are two authorities in this world, temporal and eternal, the state and the Church, creates a healthy and creative tension when there is harmonious cooperation between them. But when the state turns secular and dismissive of the teaching of the Church and of Christ—as has been happening in Canada since the late nineteen sixties—conditions will force Catholics to choose the eternal verities above and, if necessary, oppose the temporal politics of the day.

Catholics today

Until very recent days English-Canadian Catholics numbered so few that they were practically invisible. How could it be otherwise? Canada, while a huge landmass, was sparsely populated except along the St. Lawrence River, where one part was known as English and Protestant and the other as French and Catholic. The expansion westward, across the prairies and into and across the mountains, did not occur until the late nineteenth century. Meanwhile the Catholics living in the eastern region of the Maritimes, who settled there at the beginning of that century, remained stationary, and moreover looked more for inspiration to Boston and the New England states than to central Canada.

Until the middle of the twentieth century the two language groups continued to look upon themselves by and large as either English and Protestant, or French and Catholic. It was only in the post-World-War-II period that mass immigration on the one hand and political-religious changes on the other caused the demographic-religious shift within the Catholic community to become visible. Protestants in English-Canada were being outnumbered by Catholic immigrants from European countries and later also from Asia, especially the Philippines, while French-

Canadian Catholics from 1960 onward saw themselves increasingly as Quebeckers pre-occupied with building a state and less concerned with their Catholicism. Meanwhile their numbers declined while those of English Canada rose.

Let me illustrate the relative insignificance of English-Canadian Catholics in the earlier period and the shift which has taken place in the later one.

In an Advent 1999 pastoral letter entitled"Our Yesterday and our Today," Aloysius Cardinal Ambrozic presented some figures on the growth of the Archdiocese of Toronto. In 1900, Toronto, which then included what is now the Diocese of St. Catherines, had 45 parishes and 65,000 Catholics. These constituted 12 percent of the overall population in the area. In 1999 the Archdiocese had 225 parishes with a million-and-a-half Catholics, who formed some 35 percent of the area's population.

In 1900 it had 27 Catholic elementary schools and seven academies (elementary and high school combined); in 1999 it had 446 elementary schools and 80 high schools.

In 1900 there were four religious orders of women and four of men; in 1999 there were 47 orders of women and 34 orders of men. In 1900 Mass was celebrated in Latin with homilies in English, French, and occasionally Italian; in 1999 the Holy Eucharist was celebrated in 29 languages every Sunday.

As for Church attendance, the pastoral letter stated: "The regular Sunday Mass attendance has ceased falling since 1994; according to independent statistical evidence, it stands at 33 percent; we must add also that the percentage of Catholics attending Mass twice or three times a month has risen from five percent to 12 percent in the past five years."

Contrast this to Montreal in Quebec which also claimed

1.5 million Catholics in 1999. It had, as yet, a much higher number of priests and religious than Toronto. But the number of practising Catholics had dropped so much that by the late nineties it was between seven and eight percent only.

Another comparison is that of schools. In Quebec, Catholic schools ceased to exist in 1998. With the Quebec bishops' consent, the constitutional guarantees for such schools in the B.N.A. Act of 1867— reaffirmed in the federal constitutional changes of 1981-2—were removed on the initiative of the Quebec government, with the cooperation of Jean Chrétien, the French-speaking Prime Minister in Ottawa.

At the end of the twentieth century, therefore, English-speaking Catholics appear the larger of the two Catholic communities in Canada. All things remaining equal, this process will continue in the 21st century for two reasons: immigrants will continue to assimilate more thoroughly into English Canada than into Quebec; and Canada's natives or aboriginal peoples—far more numerous in Western Canada than in Quebec—have a higher birth rate than those of either English or French stock.

Does the universal Church at large know about developments in Canada? One assumes not. Rome, naturally, is well-informed, as it is about Catholics throughout the world, and the English-speaking Canadian contingent cannot but be noticed. When in 1999 Canadian bishops made their regular, five-year ad limina visits to the Holy Father, he received them in four regional groups over a period of six months: first the bishops of Quebec, then those of the Maritimes, Ontario, and Western Canada. The Pope's address to the Quebec bishops naturally was in French, while the other three were in English, although each included a paragraph or two in French in acknowledgement of French minorities in those regions. Yet, when the Vatican administration appointed a new Nuncio to Ottawa in the same year, he spoke fluent French but practically no

English, an indication perhaps that the demographic shift among Canadian Catholics has not yet been fully accommodated in Rome.

As far as historical consciousness is concerned, numbers alone tell only part of the story. The fact remains that English-speaking Catholics in Canada are strung out along a six-thousand kilometre-long strip from Newfoundland in the Atlantic to Vancouver Island in the Pacific, mostly along the American border. This makes it very difficult to "create community." Quebeckers, on the other hand, live in a geographic unit along the Northern shores of the St. Lawrence, forming a province of their own whose French language sets them apart from the rest of Canada.

When it comes to cultural achievements there is simply no comparison between English and French. English-speaking Catholics stand only at the beginning of their collective consciousness while French-Canadian Catholics have lived and savoured their history for some 350 years. Indeed, the English Catholic consciousness may never fully mature because, with the arrival of the global village, national histories and perspectives may themselves become things of the past.

At any rate, while Quebec Catholics count their local and "national" histories in the hundreds, Catholics in English-speaking Canada are just beginning: in the Maritimes and Ontario we are some 150 years old; in the West just barely one hundred. Needless to say, this paucity of history is reflected in the volume at hand. Murray Nicolson's articles—now brought together in this volume—constitute a first popular attempt at letting English-speaking Catholics know that they have a history. I am certain that in years to come more complete histories will appear and we will welcome them with open arms. But for now, let's start with what we have.

Father Alphonse de Valk, c.s.b
Publisher/editor of Catholic Insight

Acknowledgements

The articles which form the basis for this book appeared originally in *Catholic Insight*. Mrs. Doris Nicolson and Mrs. Janice Glover deserve our thanks for revising them, adding bibliographies, and providing explanatory notes where they seemed advisable. Lianne Laurence and Leeda Crawford helped in getting the illustrations in place and making further improvement to the text.

We hope that the book will provide high-school and university students, as well as the general public, with an insight into and an understanding of their Catholic heritage as Canadians. The history of the Catholic Church in Canada has many fascinating aspects, and Murray Nicolson has done a very useful service in making that history much better known than it has been.

We wish to thank everybody involved including the Ave Maria Press for printing this book at a reasonable cost.

CHAPTER ONE

CANADA PRIOR TO 1800

Frenchmen, in 1604, settled first in that portion of the Maritimes identified by the Micmac Indians as Acadie on the Bay of Fundy. Under the leadership of Samuel de Champlain, the French began subsequently to colonize the valley of the St. Lawrence, extending up the river to Quebec where, in 1608, Champlain built his first Habitation, a fortified dwelling. Moving out from Quebec, the French expanded along the Laurentian River system, claiming the land as New France.[1]

Indian Missions

From its inception, New France was Catholic, supplied by the Church with religious orders of men, and later of women, who looked after the spiritual needs of the colonists. The priestly orders, which included Recollects, Sulpicians and Jesuits, devoted considerable time and effort to the conversion of the indigenous Indian tribes. Perhaps the most ambitious group was the Jesuits, establishing mission stations among the Hurons and, in 1639, a central headquarters at Saint Marie (today Midland, Ontario), paralleling the order's colony among the Indians of Paraguay in South America.

However, in 1649 this promising venture was destroyed by the Iroquois, the tribal enemies of the Hurons and their French allies. The surviving Hurons returned to Quebec with the French in 1650, settling the area where they continue to reside today. And while the colony at St. Marie was an immediate failure, its demise provided a number of Jesuit martyrs and a pilgrimage site for future Catholic colonists in Ontario.[2]

Need for a bishop

As early as 1631, the need for a bishop in New France

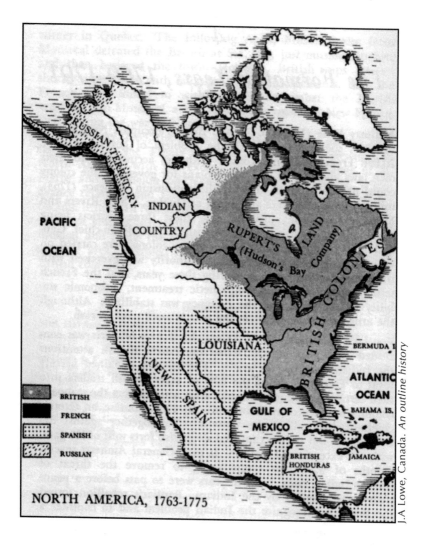

	BRITISH
	FRENCH
	SPANISH
	RUSSIAN

NORTH AMERICA, 1763-1775

RUSSIAN TERRITORY

PACIFIC OCEAN

INDIAN COUNTRY

RUPERT'S LAND (Hudson's Bay Company)

BRITISH COLONIES

BERMUDA IS.

ATLANTIC OCEAN

LOUISIANA

NEW SPAIN

GULF OF MEXICO

BAHAMA IS.

BRITISH HONDURAS

JAMAICA

J.-A Lowe, Canada. An outline history

13

was recognized. Locally, there were no regulations for religious services, there was no control of educational and charitable institutions, nor was there any direct supervision of mission activity.

By 1658 an apostolic vicariate, rather than a bishopric, was agreed upon for New France as a mission territory. Shortly after, however, in 1674, Quebec became a diocese, with François de Montmorency Laval as its first bishop. It was in 1819 that Quebec was designated an archdiocese giving it an ecclesiastical authority over the rest of British North America.[3]

Atlantic seaboard

Concurrent with the development of New France was the establishment of English colonies along the Atlantic seaboard and in Newfoundland. As a result of exploration in the far north, a British Royal Charter had been given for the incorporation of the Hudson Bay Company in 1670. But what Britain wanted was to obtain Acadia, which encompassed all of what is known as the Maritime Provinces, and New France, in its plans to expand the first British Empire.[4]

An important primary step was the acquisition of mainland Nova Scotia from France in 1713 by way of the Treaty of Utrecht. There, the British founded Halifax in 1749 as a naval base to offset the great French fortress of Louisbourg on Cape Breton Island.

The French-Catholic Acadians living in British-held territory were left relatively undisturbed. The Acadians, from the outset, had learned to be self-reliant because the French government did not readily look after their needs. When it became evident that France and Britain were doomed to clash, those Acadians who would not take an oath of loyalty to the English Crown were deported in 1755. Louisbourg fell to the British in 1758, the same year that a legislative assembly was held in Halifax in which the

Church of England was established as the state religion. And the process of expelling Acadians from Cape Breton, Prince Edward Island, and New Brunswick continued until 1763.[5]

Conquest by Britain

Catholic New France, surrounded on all sides by its Protestant enemies, suffered defeat to the British in 1760 and the territory was renamed Quebec after its principal city. Yet, considering the age, the terms of the Conquest were rather lenient, granting "the free exercise of the Roman Religion" in The Articles of Capitulation. Although Roman Catholicism was to be tolerated, the hope was that assimilation to Anglicanism would occur eventually.[6]

The Quebec Act, passed in 1774 by the British government, was enacted to resolve difficulties existing between the French Catholics and their Church, on the one hand and the British government on the other. Its purpose was to ensure Catholic loyalty in the event of any struggle that might arise against Britain in the American colonies.

The Act allowed for the practices of French civil law and feudal land tenure, legalized the collection of tithes by the Roman Catholic Church, and reaffirmed freedom of worship for Catholics—something seen as a "privilege" and one still denied in England itself in this period.

The failure to fulfil the promise of a local legislative assembly was of little consequence to French Canadians because one had never existed for them under the French regime.

Overall, the Quebec Act was the first legislation to grant religious tolerance among post-Reformation nation states and became a model of tolerance in Upper Canada and other Canadian provinces not yet formed. However, the Act was not held in the same regard by the American colonists and by English merchants in Quebec City and Montreal who resented a return to authoritarian government.[7]

United States

Following the Conquest, relations between the thirteen American colonies and Britain became increasingly strained. The war with France had been costly and England expected its colonies to assist in eradicating its vast debt. The tea acts, navigational acts, and other imposing taxes on the colonists were considered "Intolerable Acts" and fomented ill-will. Among these "intolerable" measures was the Quebec Act, which kept the Thirteen Colonies out of the Ohio Valley to the west, favouring the Montreal fur traders. In fact, the Act was denounced by the first American Congress as a violation of human rights.

Moreover, the Americans perceived a threatening implication in the denial of a local assembly in Quebec, wondering if theirs, already established, might be in peril. In addition, the strong support provided to Roman Catholicism in the terms of the Act was viewed as an oppressive gesture towards Protestantism. Consequently, the Quebec Act was one of the contributing causes of the 1776 American Revolution and the creation of a new country.

Quebec stays loyal to Britain

The fair treatment afforded French habitants by the British denied the Americans a fourteenth colony in Quebec. In the War of Independence, French Catholics, like the English Protestants who had migrated from New England to Nova Scotia, remained neutral. If anything, the anti-Catholic propaganda in the American press dissuaded Catholics in British North America from supporting the American cause.

The migration of United Empire Loyalists north to what would become Canada changed the composition of British North America. Of the 1,500 French situated in Detroit at the time of the Revolutionary War, many crossed the river to join the 660 already in Essex County, augmenting the number of French Catholics scattered across what would be Upper Canada. Included in this group were members of the Baby family, who settled in the Windsor area and later in York, and played an important role in the future development of the Catholic Church in Upper Canada.

The Loyalist groupings encompassed French Huguenots, Palatine Germans, Dutch, Swiss, Indians—particularly Mohawks from New York—blacks—freed men and escaped slaves—and those of English, Scots, and Irish background. The few United Empire Loyalists of these groups who were Catholic were Gaelic-speaking Scots and Irish. The Scottish Catholics came primarily from North Carolina or from Sir John Johnson's estate in New York's Mohawk Valley. They settled in Nova Scotia or in Upper Canada's Glengarry County (the Cornwall area today). Within a few years, the Glengarry Scots Catholics became prominent leaders in York (today Toronto).

French Revolution

Another event that had an impact on the Catholic Church in Canada was the French Revolution, which erupted in 1789 and lasted in one fashion or another until 1815. The almost-destroyed Catholic Church in France was powerless against the forces of anarchy and atheism. In 1790, the French National Assembly passed the Civil Constitution of the Clergy, a decree which confiscated the property of the Roman Catholic Church, and reorganized its structure along the lines of the new administrative system of the country. All Catholic clergy were required to take an oath of loyalty to the Constitution, making them, in effect, civil employees of the State and requiring them to repudiate the apostolic authority of the Holy Father, and simultaneously to recognize the existence of a national church distinct from Rome. In fact, all bishops and priests were to be chosen by popular vote. The clergy were divided: most bishops and about half the clergy refused to take the oath, making them refractory clergy; those who agreed were known as the constitutional clergy. But eventually even the constitutional clergy suffered in a campaign of dechristianization.

During the 'Reign of Terror' (1793-94), the leadership of the Church was hit hard, with the execution by guillotine of two archbishops, one bishop and one hundred and seventy priests. By then, some 40,000 priests and most surviving bishops had fled the country. Most of the Church land and buildings, including 400 colleges and universities and the holdings of religious orders, were expropriated by the State, never to be returned. Many churches were closed or converted into stables, with the destruction of statues, crosses, bells, and shrines. The dissolution of monasteries and convents caused the dispersement of 60,000 religious women, not a few of them ill and destitute. The constitutional priests were forced to disclaim the priesthood. Clerical celibacy was terminated. In some areas, priests were forced to marry or, if too old, were forced to adopt an elderly person or child.

In the dechristianization process, place names were stripped of any reference to the Christian past. Notre Dame Cathedral in Paris was reconsecrated to the cult of reason. The use of a new Revolutionary Calendar was enforced. It was based on twelve thirty-day months with names derived from nature, with each month composed of three ten-day weeks, abolishing Sundays and Christian feastdays, and dating Year One from the abolition of the monarchy in 1792. The new calendar system was terminated in 1805.[8]

The horrors of the French Revolution had an effect upon the New World. By 1792, the middle and upper classes and the clergy in Lower Canada regarded the occurrences in France with revulsion and realized that the France that they had honoured was disappearing. Britain was recognized as a counter-revolutionary leader. The spread of propaganda emanating from French diplomats in the United States who were inviting Quebec to join the republican movement was spurned. Various attempts were made to bring the displaced French clergy to Canada. With the exception of one or two immigrant priests, however, the invitations met with negative response. Most wanted to remain close to France in case there was a change in government. Meanwhile, the vast diocese of Quebec, ever-growing and widespread, remained insufficiently staffed to meet the spiritual and educational needs of its laity.[9]

References:

1. Marcel Trudel, *The beginnings of New France, 1524-1663* (Toronto: McLelland and Stewart, 1973), pp.1-246; Jean Daigle, "The Acadians: a people in search of a country", in *The Quebec and Acadian Diaspora in North America,* Raymond Breton and Pierre Savard, eds. (Toronto: Multicultural History Society of Ontario, 1982), pp.1-3.

2. J. Herbert Cranston, *Huronia* (Toronto: Huronia Historic Sites, 1950), pp.3-301; Harold Innis, *The fur trade in Canada* (Toronto: University of Toronto Press, 1967), pp.23-43.

3. H. H. Walsh, *The Church in the French era* (Toronto: Ryerson Press, 1966), pp.104-106.

4. *The fur trade in Canada*, pp.45-51; 189-191.

5. Daigle, op. cit., p.3.

6. Border Donaldson, *Battle for a continent:* Quebec 1759 (Toronto: Doubleday, 1973).

7. K. A. MacKirdy, J. S. Moir, V. F. Zolpvany, *Changing perspectives in Canadian history* (Toronto: Dent, 1967), pp.64-81.

8. Richard Cobb and Colin Jones, *The French Revolution: voices from a momentous epoch, 1789-1795* (New York: Viking, 1986), pp.111; 202-203.

9. J. L. Finlay and D. N. Sprague, *The structure of Canadian history* (Scarborough: Prentice-Hall, 1984), p.82.

CHAPTER TWO

THE IRISH IN NEWFOUNDLAND

What become apparent in any study of Catholicism in English Canada are the adversities its followers faced in their efforts to establish their faith in the new country. The problems stemmed partly from the religious disdain of the English majority towards those who refused to align themselves with the tenets of the Protestant Reformation, and partly from animosity towards the ethnicity of the people who professed Catholicism. These sentiments applied particularly to the Irish, whom the English regarded generally as a pariah group. In no place was the antagonism more vividly demonstrated than in Newfoundland where, unlike in Canada, the Penal Laws applied. And yet, regardless of the influence the Irish had in most of English-speaking Canada, it is in Newfoundland that the roots of Irish Catholic ethnicity run deepest.

The fisheries and the Irish

With its harsh climate and poor soil, Newfoundland was of little value for agriculture and therefore did not attract settlers. Its rich resources of fish, however, demanded labourers to accommodate the growing industry. In the late seventeenth century, migrants from Waterford, Wexford, Kilkenny, and Tipperary counties in Ireland responded and became seasonal visitors to the Island, working in the fisheries during the summer and returning home in the fall. These arrangements were inconsequential in improving the financial status of the migrant Irish workers, who were seldom paid a wage by the English merchants. Nonetheless, they presented an opportunity that otherwise would not have existed: the fisheries provided an inexpensive passage to America, making more feasible the plans of many to proceed from Newfoundland to Nova Scotia and, after two or three years of work, to gain entry into the American colonies where, it was hoped, circumstances would be better. By 1765, the fisheries in Newfoundland employed five thousand Irish, some of whom would remain and, over a period of time, create a permanent Catholic presence in Newfoundland.

It seems appropriate to look upon Newfoundland in this early period as a purgatory for the Irish. Within the framework of its judicial system, they stood little or no chance of either justice or mercy when accused of a crime. Irish Catholics were denied a defence counsel and had no way of knowing an indictment until it was read in court. On occasions when the crew on board the fishing vessels were too few to meet the demands, the Irish on-shore in Newfoundland were seized and pressed into service. If they complained they were tied to the ship's shrouds, stripped and whipped, and they received no payment for the work done.[1]

The Catholic Church at that time was an illegal institution in Britain and had great difficulty assisting the Irish in Newfoundland. Since it operated as an underground organization, its spiritual and religious role was repressed and its social activity was retarded.

Penal laws in Newfoundland

Under the English penal laws, enacted from the reign of Queen Elizabeth I (1558-1603) to that of King George III, when they were repealed in 1783, one can see the attempt to reduce 'popery' by making it impossible for a Catholic to exist, except in the lowest and most degraded state imaginable. For example, Catholics were barred from holding public office, operating schools or sitting in Parliament. They could not own property or lease it— except for ridiculously short periods of time. They could not own a horse worth more than $5. The practice of their religion was outlawed.[2]

As stated, the penal laws were applied in Newfoundland. Moreover they were augmented by local orders and practices. Catholics could not bury their dead; only an Anglican incumbent was permitted to read the service of burial and collect a fee for doing so. Aware that Catholics were practising their religion by stealth, the local authorities hunted the itinerant priests who hid, said Mass, and fled. Punishment for participation in the Mass was severe. One account refers to a Michael Keating of Harbour Main who, in 1755, was fined $50 for allowing Mass to be celebrated in his fish store. His house was demolished, his goods were seized, and he was banished from the Island.[3]

Despite the hardships, many Irish sought to remain in Newfoundland, to the dismay of local authorities. Under the guise of better "preserving the peace, preventing robberies, tumultuous assemblies, and other disorders of wicked and idle people remaining in the country during winter", Governor Palliser issued a set of official orders applicable to Newfoundland on 31 October 1764:

> That no papist servants, man or woman, shall remain at any place where they do not fish or serve during the summer proceedings;
>
> - that not more than two papist men shall dwell in one house during the winter except such as have a Protestant master;
>
> - that no papist shall keep a public house or vend liquor by retail;
>
> - that all idle and disorderly men and women be punished according to law and sent out of the Country.[4]

Socially depressed, religiously deprived, linguistically variant and culturally different, the Irish were not readily accepted or assimilated in Newfoundland. Because English law provided no assistance to them, whether in Ireland or Newfoundland, they sought some form of extralegal protection. The purpose was served through the development of Irish regional associations determined to mete out some form of justice, such as the Clear Airs from Tipperary; Whey and Yellow Bellies from Waterford; Doans or Kilkenny boys, Dadgeens from Cork; as well as Young Colts, White Boys and Black Feet. These regional identities were upheld and carried over to Newfoundland for security, often, however, exploding into faction fighting that did cause concern for the local authorities.[5]

Irish culture and the Church

Nevertheless, the Newfoundland Irish expressed a unique culture in various dialects, crafts, and traditions, particularly related to weddings and wakes, cooking, art, music, and writing, all of which are still identifiable. Gaelic, the Irish language, was commonly spoken among the Newfoundland Irish until the beginning of the nineteenth century. Its influence caused an Irish pattern of speech and a vocabulary that is still noticeable in current Newfoundland English, especially on the Avalon Peninsula.[6]

No matter what political and legal arrangements governed the practice of Catholicism in Newfoundland, Rome acted on its responsibility to the Island's Catholic population. From 1535 to 1784, Newfoundland was placed under the administration of the Bishop of Rouen, then the Bishop of Quebec and, finally, the London Vicariate. A number of itinerant priests were sent to Newfoundland; under great difficulty, and at considerable risk, they traversed the rough terrain, surreptitiously said Mass, and then moved on. These men were under the constant threat of surveillance by Protestants, who felt obliged to report their activities. One example, documented in 1755, stated: "Whereas I am informed that a Roman Catholic priest is at this time at Harbour Grace, and that he publicly read mass, which is contrary to the law and against the peace of our sovereign Lord, the King."[7]

And while good and dedicated priests struggled to bring religion to the people, their efforts were occasionally undermined by the scandalous behaviour of a few vagabonds. There are accounts of one priest living in a sinful relationship with the wife of a Protestant man; of others, in drunken fits, making sport of the Catholic religion; and of another revealing openly, from one harbour to the next, the contents of what he heard in confession. Without local ecclesiastic control, it was impossible to harness the activity of these independent and restive clergy.

In 1784 with the repeal of the English penal laws, "liberty of conscience" was proclaimed in Newfoundland and Catholics were able to practice their religion openly, provided it was done quietly.[8] That same year Rome appointed an Irish Franciscan, James Louis O'Donel, as Superior of the Mission of the Island of Newfoundland, and the first Catholic chapel was built. O'Donel oversaw a small group of mostly Irish priests who sailed from one outport to the next. The priests were welcomed by the inhabitants of those forlorn coastal settlements which had been spiritually deprived. Thousands converted to Catholicism over the next decade because of their ministry. Moreover O'Donel's presence effected law and order among the Irish settlers, and his diocesan statutes, issued in 1801, helped to bring under control those priests who had created scandal. O'Donel was succeeded in 1806 by Patrick Lambert from Ireland, an action which affirmed the continuity of Irish clergy in Newfoundland. Because of this close association with Ireland, contacts with the Diocese of Quebec were minimal.

By the early nineteenth century about half of Newfoundland's population was Roman Catholic, and the Church was short of priests and funds. Between 1817 and 1829, under the third Vicar Apostolic, Thomas Scallan, the number of priests available to serve the needs of the Island and Labrador ranged from seven to ten. The arrival of Scallan's replacement, Michael Anthony Fleming, another Irish Franciscan, signalled change. Fleming divided Newfoundland into regular missions and obtained more priests from Ireland to expand the work of the Church. Two orders of nuns came from Ireland, the Sisters of the Presentation in 1833 and the Sisters of Mercy in 1842. They set up boarding schools, an orphanage, and a home for working girls.

Although by mid-nineteenth century the Catholic population was no longer an absolute majority, it was sufficient to warrant a formal diocesan structure. Fleming became titular Bishop of Newfoundland in 1847, with another Irish Franciscan, John Thomas Mullock, as coadjutor. One of the first projects undertaken was the construction of the cathedral at St. John's, which was consecrated in 1855. The following year the diocese was divided; John Dalton became Bishop of Harbour Grace, with a jurisdiction that included the whole of the Labrador coast, while the Newfoundland Diocese fell under Bishop John Mullock. Mullock continued to promote institution building and charitable and educational work. He directed efforts towards the training of native Newfoundlanders for the priesthood by establishing in St. John's, in 1856, St. Bonaventure College as a diocesan seminary.[9] The Christian Brothers arrived from Ireland in 1857 to begin their program of educating Catholic youths. It was not, however, until the twentieth century that St. Clare's Mercy Hospital was opened. (It was closed in 1995.)

Conditions for Newfoundland's Catholics, predominantly Irish, gradually improved as the laws changed. Certainly benefits were gained when Catholics received the power to vote and, finally, to sit in the assembly and on the Legislative Council. The creation of a Catholic school system aided the progress of the people. The struggle to obtain the rights of their religion, however, was hard. Could Newfoundland Catholics in the late 1800s have envisaged, a century later, the breakdown and elimination of all that they had worked for to educate their children in the faith and provide the means of supporting and nurturing their families?

References:

1. C. J. Houston, W. J. Smyth, *Irish emigration and Canadian settlement* (Toronto: University of Toronto Press, 1990), pp.16-17; 67; 69; 336

2. C. J. Byrne, ed., *Gentlemen-bishops and faction fighters*: the letters of bishops O'Donel, Lambert, Scallan, and other Irish missionaries (St. John's: Jesperson Press, 1984), pp.4-5.

3.Michael J. *McCarthy,The Irish in Newfoundland*, 1623-1800 (St. John's Nfld.: Creative Printers & Publishers, 1982), p.22.

4. Ibid., p.28.

5. P. O'Donnell, *The Irish faction fighters of the 19th century* (Anvil Books, 1975).

6. George Casey, "Irish culture in Newfoundland", in C. J. Byrne, M. Harry, *ThLamh an eise* (Halifax: Nimbus, 1986), pp.203-228.

7. Op. cit., p.20.

8. Byrne, pp.39-52.

9. John S. Moir, *The Church in the British era: from the British conquest to Confederation* (Toronto: McGraw-Hill, 1972), pp.32; 157.

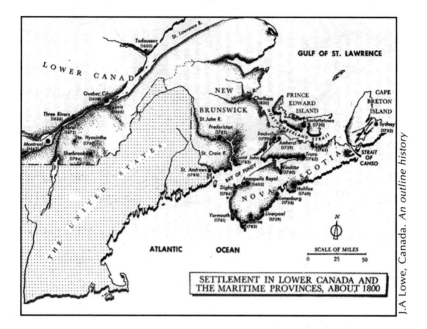

Map labels (clockwise): Tadoussac (1600), St. Lawrence R., GULF OF ST. LAWRENCE, LOWER CANADA, Quebec City (1608), Chatham (1800), PRINCE EDWARD ISLAND, CAPE BRETON ISLAND, NEW BRUNSWICK, St. John R., Fredericton (1783), Charlottetown, Sydney (1752), Three Rivers (1634), St. Hyacinthe (1748), Montreal (1642), Sherbrooke (1794), St. Croix, Grand John (1783), Sackville (1771), Amherst (1759), Truro (1765), Shubenacadie (1762), STRAIT OF CANSO, NORTHUMBERLAND STRAIT, St. Andrews (1783), BAY OF FUNDY, Windsor (1760), Annapolis Royal (1605), Digby (1784), NOVA SCOTIA, Halifax (1749), Lunenburg (1753), Yarmouth (1761), Liverpool (1759), (1783), THE UNITED STATES, ATLANTIC OCEAN, N, SCALE OF MILES, 0 25 50, SETTLEMENT IN LOWER CANADA AND THE MARITIME PROVINCES, ABOUT 1800

J.A Lowe, Canada. An outline history

CHAPTER THREE
THE IRISH AND SCOTS IN THE MARITIMES

Acadians

Today Prince Edward Island's people are divided equally as far as the Catholic and Protestant populations are concerned. Within the Catholic segment are the Acadians, who make up twelve percent of the provincial total. Most of the Islanders continue to depend upon the soil and the sea for a livelihood.

Currently in New Brunswick, the Acadians form approximately one-third of that province's population. Following the American War of Independence, United Empire Loyalists amalgamated with the already settled Protestant factions, swinging the balance away from a Catholic majority. In addition to good farmland in the St. John River

Valley, New Brunswick's abundant forests supplied a lumber industry that supported many people.

Across the Bay of Fundy, Nova Scotia, with mining, agriculture, and industry, has a population that is thirty-seven percent Catholic, of whom eight percent are Acadian, and among whom only three and a half percent are French-speaking.[1]

The Scots in the Maritimes

One of the largest ethnic groups in the Maritimes is the Scots, originating primarily from the Highlands and Islands of Scotland. They brought with them a rich oral culture in the Gaelic tongue, a passion for ghost stories and folklore, and a strong adherence to religious principles. Most were dispossessed tenant farmers whose clannish instincts caused them to emigrate from Scotland en masse.

The beginnings in 1773

Scottish immigration of some consequence really began when the ship Hector dropped anchor at Pictou, Nova Scotia, in 1773. Having undergone an arduous crossing of the Atlantic, during which eighteen children died, the Scots Highlanders were dismayed to see trees crowding down to the edge of the water and approximately sixteen families, who had arrived in 1767 with the Philadelphia Company, housed in crude shelters. Seventy-eight of the Hector passengers remained in Pictou and, enduring great hardship and hunger, ensured the settlement of the area. They were joined by a second body of settlers in 1783-84, comprised primarily of disbanded soldiers whose Highland regiments had been on garrison duty in Halifax and Quebec or had been fighting in the American colonies. Included in this group was a number of Catholic Highlanders, many of whom later moved to the Nova Scotian town of Antigonish.[2]

The next large contingent of settlers emigrated from the Western Isles of Scotland. This group of Catholics disembarked from the ship Dunkeld at Pictou, in 1791, where by this time Presbyterianism was well established. This new group was practically destitute, and the inhabitants of Pictou, themselves in dire straits, could provide only meagre help. Consequently an appeal for aid was made to the colonial government. Reverend James MacGregor, the Presbyterian minister, requested his followers to treat the Catholic newcomers with courtesy. Nonetheless he was distressed by their actions and concerned about the impact they might have on his flock:

> Much of their time was spent in naughty diversions, jestings which are not convenient nor decent, in telling extravagant stories of miracles done by priests, and absurd tales about ghosts, witches, fairies, etc. The minds of the Protestant Highlanders, being partly tinctured with these superstitions before the arrival of the Roman Catholics, were less prepared to resist their influence than the minds of more reasoning and sceptical Christians.[3]

At the prompting of Father A. MacEachern, many of these Catholics moved eastward to Antigonish and Cape Breton.

More immigration in 1801

In 1801 and 1802 other large groups of Catholic Highlanders arrived in Nova Scotia, many of whom joined their coreligionists in the Antigonish area. Three hundred and seventy left from the Scottish island of Barra, where they were accustomed to the fisheries. At their request, they were located "on Pictou Island and the shores opposite, for the convenience of carrying on the Herring and other shore fisheries, with which that coast abounds."[4] While some of the Catholic Highlanders were involved in the fisheries, others engaged in shipbuilding, small manufacture, and merchandising. Most, however, were uninterested in commercial activity, seeking rather to obtain land.

Lord Thomas Selkirk, a colonizer who aided in the

immigration of 2,000 destitute Scots, observed that they tended to make money in the summer months and then waste it during winter in idleness and drink. A few took to farming, but those Scots who were Catholic were not well received by the resident Methodists and the New Light People (a group separated from the Congregationalists). Moreover, they did not speak English and, to make matters worse, the Scots Gaelic differed in pronunciation, word order and meaning from area to area and with that spoken by the Irish. Consequently, conversation was slow. But most itinerant priests were able to accommodate and hear confessions in either the Irish or Scots Gaelic as they moved among their flock. Nevertheless, in a sizeable sector of the Maritimes, Gaelic was the language commonly heard in homes and on the streets of many villages and towns, which made communication among the groups difficult to achieve.[5]

Catholic Highland Scots' settlements centred more particularly in the eastern portion of the Maritimes, in Antigonish, Prince Edward Island, and along the west shore of Cape Breton. While priests accompanied the later waves of immigration, their numbers were insufficient to serve the needs of the scattered Catholic populations. As a responsive measure, the Bishop of Quebec issued commissions to laymen to perform marriages and baptisms. The Scots were poor and unable to afford either altar cloths or albs, and it was said that only a Scots priest would consent to say Mass under those conditions.

While the fervour of their faith might have been great, the Highlanders suffered a loss of religious attention. Beginning with a small log chapel, the first Catholic parish was established in 1793 at Arisaig near Antigonish. Considering that its first pastor, Father James MacDonald, had also to serve Pictou and the western part of Cape Breton, it is not surprising that he succumbed to such a heavy load and died in 1807. Two other Scots priests took up the burden, covering Prince Edward Island, the Gulf

Shore and Cape Breton. To compensate for the lack of Gaelic-speaking priests, a number of young men from Prince Edward Island and eastern Nova Scotia was sent to study for the priesthood in Quebec, but only two were ordained.[6]

Bishop Plessis of Quebec

Bishop Plessis of Quebec, under whose jurisdiction the Maritimes remained until 1817, made two pastoral visits, in 1812 and 1815, when he learned how deprived of spiritual needs were his Gaelic-speaking flock. He was disturbed by the lack of church furnishings in Prince Edward Island. One church had no missal, another used a tin cup for a chalice. At St. Andrew's, dogs were running loose in the church. Moreover, the Scots women wore dresses with plunging necklines. What shocked him most was a custom of the Scots falling to the floor and crawling to the altar rail during the distribution of communion. In his opinion, things were never quite as bad in Upper Canada. On the other hand, the Acadians in Cape Breton beautified their churches.

Bishop Plessis appointed Father Remi Gaulin, who would later became the Bishop of Kingston in Upper Canada, as first pastor to St. Ninian's in Antigonish in 1815. Father Gaulin, who also ministered in Margaree and Cheticamp in Inverness County, was disturbed by the behaviour of his young Scots charges. In a letter to Bishop Plessis in 1815, Father Gaulin wrote:

> I take the liberty earnestly to beseech your Lordship to issue a special mandate against drinking on Sundays and at funerals, and regulating the weddings, which are among the Scotch, as scandalous as their funerals, and specifying the public penances to be imposed upon the transgressors. Your Lordship may rest assured that nothing less can put a stop to evils at which even Protestants are shocked. [7]

Father Gaulin was hindered by a lack of Gaelic, but it

seems he expressed the same complaints about his young French-speaking Acadian charges. In the next decade, Bishop Angus MacEachern, whose missionary service was more extensive than that of any other of the pioneer priests, reported:

> The Catholics of these counties are well attached to their Religion. And Govt. is vastly kind to us. The Acadian French, in the Gulf, are the most correct Christians in these parts. Our Highlanders are staunch Catholics.[8]

And what of these staunch Catholics? The Highlanders carried with them their old hatreds, particularly toward the Campbells who, they believed, raised their status by trickery and deception and placing obstacles in the path of other free-hearted clans like the MacDonalds, MacLeans, and MacGregors. They also brought with them a rich heritage of household arts, games, dances, music, and unwritten literature. A favourite Gaelic proverb, thig crioch air an t-sao-ghas, is interpreted as "An end will come to the world, but music and love will endure." However, just as few books were printed in Gaelic so that oral literature was left unwritten, so too Highland music was entirely unrecorded. Songs accompanied work. For example, the women sang a milling frolic as they beat woven cloth to raise its nap. But songs did not spring only from folk memory; many were composed in the Maritimes. The bagpipes were the instrument of the Highlands, and pipers were among the early settlers. They were considered suitable and, indeed, almost indispensable at any occasion of celebration, or rite of passage. And the pipers' skills were graced by those of the fiddlers.

The coming of the Irish

British imperial policy not only promoted Scottish immigration, but it also caused that of the Irish. Among the first settlers in Nova Scotia was a group of Irish Catholic soldiers serving under the command of a Colonel T.

Hierlihy, himself not a Catholic. After the evacuation of New York, the regiment was sent to Halifax and then to Prince Edward Island. Hierlihy and his soldiers were given a sizeable grant of land on both sides of Antigonish Harbour. As veterans, they received considerable government assistance in setting up their homesteads.

Included in the passenger lists of Scottish Catholic immigrants was a number of Irish during the period of intense emigration from 1815 to 1821. By the late 1820s, the Nova Scotia government discouraged immigration because it was unprepared to cope with the destitute and diseased condition of arriving passengers, particularly the Irish. Consequently, many of the new Irish arrivals moved on to the United States. And this pattern of movement to urban centres that could better support them, particularly to Halifax, continued. While some were able to lead comfortable lives, many of them worked under wretched conditions, and lived hungry in substandard homes. Disaster needed no explanation and was accepted without complaint, most likely because of the treatment they had endured in Ireland under the British. They were not, however, much better received in the New World.

The first of several Passenger Acts was passed by the British government in 1803 to safeguard emigrants to British North America from the unscrupulous tactics of ship owners and to gain control over emigration practices. It stipulated the number of passengers, the space to be provided, the requirement for medical attention, and the provisions to be furnished, all of which were to be enforced by customs officers. Newfoundland and Labrador were exempt from the regulations. There were many violations and, consequently, poor Irish found their way across the Atlantic to Nova Scotia which was ill-prepared to cope with the steady flow of immigrants. Richard John Uniacke, Attorney-General for Nova Scotia, addressing the Select Committee on Emigration in 1826, pointed to the failure of the Acts. He contended that the Irish, given a bed and "pork and flour", as the passenger regulations required, and to which they were unaccustomed, became sick. On the other hand, the Irish man sailing the cheapest route to Newfoundland "gets no more than his breadth and length upon the deck of a ship and he has no more provisions than a few herrings, and he comes out a hearty man."[9]

The Irish outnumbered the United Empire Loyalists, who by the 1830s dominated the social and political life of the colonies. But the Irish, like the Scots, never received the assistance the Loyalists got. Pushed to the periphery, they were noted for drunkenness, rowdyism, and crime. Generally speaking, they were pessimistic; having lost faith in any temporal improvement, they sought consolation in their religion.

In extending its hegemony the British Government was often rather cruel in its treatment of the populations in Ireland and Scotland. While Ireland had been an English colony for centuries and suffered subjugation, the Highland Scots, many of them Catholic, faced banishment in the 'clearances', beginning in the late eighteenth century when men were replaced by sheep for economic gain. Similarly, the Acadians had been removed from the Maritimes by the British between 1755 and 1757. But by 1800, the Acadians were found again, chiefly in three locations: along the upper St. John River and the east coast of New Brunswick, and in Prince Edward Island where they comprised half the Island's population.

Catholics and the State

At the political level there had been a number of events that affected the participation of Catholics in the social sphere. In 1757, the Nova Scotia Council declared that no 'popish recusant' could vote in the approaching elections. With the repeal of the Penal Laws in 1784, Catholicism was accepted as a legal, viable religion, so Scots, Irish, Acadian, and Micmac Indian Catholics could worship God in their own rite, and emancipation of Catholics would soon follow. By 1789,

Catholics were allowed to vote in Nova Scotia, but not until 1810 in New Brunswick.

Although allowed to vote, Catholics were excluded from public office because of the Test Act, which was passed in 1673 and was in force in Great Britain until 1829. This Act required holders of public office under the Crown to make the 'Declaration against Transubstantiation' and to receive the Eucharist according to the usage of the Church of England. In 1820, Cape Breton was annexed to Nova Scotia and was allowed two representatives to the Nova Scotia House of Assembly. Two men of Irish origin were selected: R.J. Uniacke, Jr., a Protestant, and Lawrence Kavanagh. As a Catholic, under the Test Act, Kavanagh could not take his seat. However, his cause was taken up by Uniacke and Thomas C. Haliburton, and, in 1823, Kavanagh was granted the right to his seat once he had taken an oath of loyalty which omitted the anti-Catholic clauses. Pleased with the Colonial Office's repudiation of the Test and Corporation Acts, the Nova Scotia Assembly voted to remove the declaration against Catholic beliefs included in the oath of office. This, however, was nullified when Catholic emancipation was accepted in Great Britain and extended to the whole Empire in 1829. And while improvements in the political status of Catholics occurred in the Maritimes, they were often countered by a bitter resurgence of anti-papal sentiment.[10]

The institutional Church in the vast area was weak, and it had to struggle to meet the spiritual needs of a laity that was dispersed over large areas and divided along ethnic and linguistic lines. What a momentous occasion it must have been when Bishop Pierre Denaut made a pastoral visit in 1803, the first since that conducted by Bishop Jean Baptiste de Saint-Vallier of Quebec in 1695! The purpose of the trip was to confirm the members of the laity, and hundreds received the sacrament in Cape Breton, New Brunswick, Nova Scotia, and Prince Edward Island. At

Arichat alone, one thousand and sixty-two were confirmed, almost the entire population.

Civil recognition

Since the time of the conquest, Catholic Church officials in Quebec had been in a precarious position, as the Church of England sought to establish itself in Lower Canada. Bishop Plessis, who succeeded Denaut, proved to be an astute statesman. In recognition for loyalty to the King, particularly during the War of 1812, Plessis received civil and legal recognition to his title from the imperial government, paving the way for the division of the Diocese of Quebec. During 1815, the year in which Plessis made his second pastoral visit to the Maritimes, he wrote to the Vatican concerning the division. Two years later, Rome named Edmund Burke Vicar Apostolic of Nova Scotia (excluding Cape Breton). The fact that Burke made an independent visit to Rome to report the Church's depressed condition in the Atlantic provinces and to request approval for his appointment as Vicar Apostolic displeased Plessis. Nonetheless, Burke was consecrated by Plessis in Quebec in 1818. Meanwhile Plessis interceded with Rome and the British government to obtain another suffragan and vicar apostolic for the rest of the Maritimes. In 1819, Angus MacEachern was made suffragan to Plessis, with jurisdiction over Prince Edward Island and New Brunswick. Two years later he was consecrated by Plessis to the missionary episcopacy to rule Prince Edward Island and Cape Breton.

While these arrangements should have strengthened the Church, they failed to do so initially because of Scots-Irish ethnic clashes. Bishop Burke died in 1820. Because his coadjutor refused to serve, the administration of his district fell to his nephew, Father John Carroll, a twenty-two-year-old who had been ordained for only six months. The seminary was dissolved and church building in Halifax halted. Funds ran out and the older Irish priests resented Carroll's authority. The arrival from Scotland to Antigonish in 1822 of some three hundred Highlanders with the Gaelic-speaking Father William Fraser prompted a local "revolt" of Scots against their Irish priest.

Bishop MacEachern became Father Fraser's patron and, as a consequence, Fraser was appointed Burke's successor in Nova Scotia and consecrated some six and a half years after Burke's death. Bishop Fraser, however, refused to live among the Irish Catholics in Halifax, preferring the company of his fellow Scots in Antigonish; he left an Irish vicar general to administer in Halifax. In 1842, Fraser was made titular bishop of Halifax and an Irishman, William Walsh, his coadjutor. The two men were not on speaking terms, and trouble was avoided only in 1844 by transferring Fraser to the new bishopric in Arichat, which encompassed Antigonish and Cape Breton, and making Walsh Bishop of Halifax. Thus the Scottish and Irish elements were split.

In the same period New Brunswick was separated from Prince Edward Island. Bishop Bernard Donald McDonald, a native of the Island, who had succeeded MacEachern in 1837, continued as Bishop there, while an Irishman, William Dollard, became the first Bishop of New Brunswick.

By 1850, a large, loyal, and devout Catholic population was well established in the Maritimes. Economic stability because of timber, fish, and agricultural trade supported the rapid expansion of educational institutions and church buildings. The people benefited from the founding of St. Mary's College in Halifax, ironically by Bishop Fraser who had refused to live there. The opening of a seminary at Arichat by a native Nova Scotian, Bishop Colin Francis Mackinnon, provided the priests needed for the whole of the Maritimes. It was chartered in 1866 as St. Francis Xavier University. Located in Antigonish, the university sponsored the Antigonish Movement that was to gain world renown in Catholic social action in the twentieth century.

Acknowledging the need to recognize the Acadians' identity, the Church created a second diocese in Chatham New Brunswick. The foundation of a petit séminaire later evolved into St. Joseph's College, which stimulated the revival of Acadian culture. Consequently the Catholic fabric woven into the Maritimes was a blend of Scots, Irish, and Acadians.[11]

References:

1. J. Bartlet Brebner, *Canada: a modern history* (Lansing: University of Michigan Press, 1970), pp.168-205.

2. D. Campbell, R. A. MacLean, *Beyond the Atlantic roar: a study of the Nova Scotian Scots* (Toronto: McLelland & Stewart, 1974), pp.16; 36-38.

3. *Ibid.*, p.41.

4. *Ibid.*, pp.42-43.

5. Charles W. Dunn, *Highland settler: a portrait of the Scottish Gael in Nova Scotia* (Toronto: University of Toronto Press, 1953), pp.74-79.

6. R. MacLean, "The Highland Catholic tradition in Canada", in W. Stanford Reid, ed., *The Scottish Tradition in Canada* (Toronto: McLelland & Stewart, 1976), pp.93-117.

7. A. A. Johnston, *A history of the Catholic Church in Eastern Nova Scotia* (Toronto: Longmans, 1960), p.325.

8. Ibid., p.419.

9. William Forbes Adams, *Ireland and Irish emigration to the New World from 1815 to the Famine* (Baltimore, Geneological Pub. Corp., 1980), p.153.

10 J. S. Moir, *The Church in the British era*, p.138; Terrence M. Punch "'Gentle as the snow on a rooftop': The Irish in Nova Scotia to 1830", in Robert O'Driscoll and Lorna Reynolds, eds., *The untold story: the Irish in Canada* (Toronto: Celtic Arts of Canada, 1988), p.226.

11. See in general: A. A. MacKenzie, *The Irish in Cape Breton* (Antigonish: Formac Pub., 1979); J. Brian Hanington, *Every popish person: the story of Roman Catholicism in Nova Scotia and the church of Halifax,1604-1984* (Archdiocese of Halifax, 1984).

CHAPTER FOUR

ALEXANDER MACDONELL

Upper Canada's first bishop

One of the most influential figures in the advancement of the Catholic Church in English-speaking Canada was Alexander Macdonell. As the first Catholic bishop of Upper Canada, he was a remarkable prelate, well qualified to administer a missionary diocese during the pioneer period of this province. A seemingly self-righteous and authoritative Highland Scot, Macdonell was to base the future of the Church and laity on his loyalty to the British Crown, his alliance with the Upper Canada Tory faction, and a coterie of Catholic and Protestant "Compact" friends who held the reins of power.

Alexander Macdonell

Alexander Macdonell was born in Scotland in 1762. Despite the penal laws the Macdonell clan members clung to their Catholic faith. Because of the anti-Catholic Gordon Riots in 1780 and the renewal of anti-Catholic sentiment, primary Catholic education was non-existent in Scotland, and it seems likely that Macdonell received his early education at home. His parents sent him to the Scots College in Paris and then to the Royal Scots College at Valladolid, Spain, where he was ordained to the priesthood in 1787.

Shortly after Father Macdonell's return to the Highlands, many of the tenant farmers were being ejected and were undergoing terrible hardships. The restrictions of the emigration acts did not allow them to leave the country. Macdonell went to Glasgow to seek employment for his laity in the factories. However, mindful of the Riots and fearful for the safety of their operations if Catholics were hired, factory owners were hesitant to employ the displaced Highlanders, but relented in their need for labourers.

For two years, Father Macdonell lived among his people in Glasgow. He said Mass and preached in English and Gaelic without fear of the anti-Catholic rabble or the courts, yet he was canny enough to post a guard at the door when he was involved in those activities. But with an economic depression in 1794 his Highlanders were once again out of work. Many were forced to enlist in the British army to survive, but had to declare themselves Protestant before being accepted. In counteraction, Macdonell conceived the idea of forming Highlanders into a single regiment wherein they could find employment, retain their religion, and still show their loyalty.[1]

At a meeting of Catholics at Fort Augustus in the Scottish Highlands in 1794, an address was made to King George III. Father Macdonell offered to raise a Catholic corps, the Glengarry Fencible Regiment, under the command of Macdonell of Glengarry, with himself as chaplain. Britain, at war with Napoleon, received the deputation and, contrary to the existing Test Act, Father Macdonell was gazetted chaplain in the first Catholic regiment raised since the Reformation. The regiment was dispatched first to the Isle of Guernsey, and in 1798 was sent to Ireland, during the rebellion there. Because of Father Macdonnell's presence among his soldiers, the excesses generally committed against the Irish peasantry by other regiments and the native Yeomanry Corps were prevented. Macdonell was appalled to find that most of the Catholic chapels of Wicklow, Carlow, and Wexford had been turned into stables. Once they were cleaned and restored, he encouraged the return of clergy and congregation, "most of whom had been driven into the mountains and bogs."[2]

Having served its purpose, the Glengarry Highlander regiment was disbanded in 1802 and the rank and file faced a bleak future without employment. Father Macdonell attempted to gain some compensation for the services put forth by his men and entered into negotiations with Henry Addington, the Prime Minister, on their behalf.

The Imperial Government offered options in land settlements: one in Trinidad and another on the shores of Canada's Lake Superior. Macdonell rejected both. In his opinion the climate of Trinidad was unsuitable for men of his ilk, and the land around Lake Superior too barren for farming. The third offer was acceptable: to settle his highlanders in the Glengarry district of Upper Canada, with a grant of two hundred acres for every soldier in his regiment.[3]

Scots in Upper Canada

Highland Scots had moved into Upper Canada after the American War of Independence. When the King's Royal Regiment of New York and the Royal Highland Emigrants were disbanded in 1784, the men were given lots along the St. Lawrence River and lake fronts. Another group of Catholic Scots from the New York Mohawk Valley settled in the western section of Glengarry and around St. Andrew's in Stormont between 1780 and 1784. (Note: In 1786 another Rev. Alexander Macdonnel [Scotus] brought his parish from Knoydart in Scotland to the area around St. Raphael in Glengarry where he built the "blue chapel". As one of the first non-French priests in Upper Canada, he served until 1803, dying on his way to Montreal to seek medical attention.) It was to this particular Highland Scottish enclave in Upper Canada that Father Macdonell sent his soldier clansmen with their families in 1803, followed by a second wave in 1804.

Father Macdonell first contacted Bishop J.O. Plessis, coadjutor to Bishop Denaut of Quebec, to advise him of his arrival, and then went to Longueuil, where he received from Bishop Denaut the ecclesiastical authority to act as a priest in Upper Canada. With a glowing introduction, Macdonell proceeded to York (today Toronto) to secure the land grants promised his flock in Britain. While there he developed a close friendship with Upper Canada

Lieutenant-Governor Hunter. From that period, Macdonell utilized his personal loyalty to win the support of succeeding lieutenants-governor to gain advantages for himself, his clergy, teachers, and flock.

When Father Macdonell arrived in Upper Canada, there were three Catholic churches and two priests: Father Fitzsimmons at St. Andrew's, who departed the province within a year, and the French-speaking Father Marchand at Sandwich, who served the French settlement around what is now Windsor. From the mission of St. Raphael in Glengarry, Macdonell visited the Catholics throughout the whole of Upper Canada, an expanse that ranged from the provincial line at Coteau du Lac to Lake Superior. He travelled through country without roads or bridges, on horseback, wagon, canoe, or on foot, carrying the essentials for the Mass.

Bishop Macdonell

In recognition of his singular missionary work, Macdonell was made vicar general by Bishop Plessis in 1807. On 12 January 1819 he was appointed bishop, and consecrated by Bishop Plessis on 31 December 1820. The title gave him a certain stature in his relationship with the military establishment and the elite, as well as a hierarchical position exceeding that of the Anglican Archdeacon John Strachan of York. More significantly, it paved the way to his appointment as bishop of Kingston when Upper Canada was made a single diocese in 1826, independent of Quebec.

Macdonell was surrounded by a group of loyal and influential Highland Scottish Catholics. Among his friends were four prominent members of Clan Donald, which included the Cadet families of Abercholder, Collochie, Greenfield, and Leek. Alexander Macdonell (Collochie) was a member of the Legislative Assembly and Council, a magistrate, and Sheriff of the Home District. He was also a land speculator, a member of the Masonic Order, and holder of a pew for his wife in St. James Anglican Church in York. However, it was he along with others who founded the first Catholic church in York, St. Paul's.

Family influence

The group of tight-knit, wealthy Scots Catholics was of great assistance to Bishop Macdonell in obtaining land grants. Macdonell sat on the Legislative Council from 1831 until the time of his death, and in that position maintained constant contact with those families. Furthermore he could rely on the assistance of various members of the influential Baby family in York and in Windsor. One in particular was James Baby, an executive and legislative councillor, lieutenant of the County of Kent, judge of the Court of Common Pleas, and inspector general of accounts for Upper Canada. Macdonell could also count on the support of the Catholic faction of a well-established Loyalist family, the Jones. The interlocking marriage relationships of that family gave Macdonell leverage with the Protestant Compact families including the Sherwoods, Boultons, Elmsleys, Crawfords and MacNabs. Through friendship with the military elite, the governors, and well-placed men like John Galt, Macdonell achieved the material advancement of his Church, specifically in land grants and pensions.

Although differing on points of religion, Macdonell and the Anglican Bishop Strachan maintained excellent terms. As staunch Tories, both sat in Council. Competition was minimal. For example, Macdonell did not disagree with the concept of the Clergy Reserves, which set aside land for the benefit of Protestant churches and particularly the Anglican church; he just wanted a share in them.

Beyond what existed in 1804, Macdonell gained lands for the Catholic Church and established missions in York, Niagara, Peterborough, Prescott, Bytown, Belleville, Kingston, Perth, Cobourg, Port Hope, Dundas, Guelph, St.

Thomas, London, and St. Catharines. He sent missionaries from main centres into the hinterland to make contact with isolated Catholic families. He established a seminary at St. Raphael's in Glengarry to educate priests and the sons of prosperous families, and in 1838 built Regiopolis College in Kingston. In 1830 he founded a diocesan newspaper, *The Catholic*, printed in Kingston, and later re-established with the same format and under the same name between 1841 to 1844 in Hamilton.[4]

Changes in population

Meanwhile, the Catholic population began to change from Scottish Catholic in Glengarry and a detached French block at Sandwich to encompass a rapidly growing Irish element. By 1834 there were 52,428 Catholics; approximately 10,000 were Scots, 8,000 French, and 34,000 Irish. The Scots remained dominant in Glengarry; the French, still dominant in Windsor, had also moved into Ottawa (Bytown) and Penetanguishene from Drummond Island; and the predominant Irish settled in the central area of Upper Canada. Ethnicity contributed to divisiveness.

Bishop Macdonell failed to divide his massive diocese into local deaneries, to call a synod of priests, or to establish Church courts. It took years before he finally appointed a coadjutor, even though well-qualified and trained personnel were available. Instead he depended almost solely upon the force of his own personality and exclusive friends to maintain control.

Meanwhile his relationship with the growing Irish population became problematic. In Macdonell's evaluation they were lukewarm Catholics, semi-barbarous in comparison to his Catholic Highlanders. But he could compliment them for their good points, even at the expense of his own kin: "As you and I know well the difference between the liberality of open-hearted Irish men and close-fisted Scotsmen."[5]

His opinion of the Irish, however, was swayed some-
what by that of his episcopal superiors. Bishop Plessis
called them the "scum of the population." Bishop
Lartrique labelled them an unwanted race, disloyal, and
radically anti-British (in a period when the Church in
France was seeking British accommodation).

Perhaps the disrespectful behaviour of some Irish towards
Macdonell could be attributed to the fact that the bishop
seemed to court the favour of the Orange Order, arch-enemy
of Irish Catholics: "It is with no small gratification that I here

Guelph, 1827. Showing MacDonell Street

acknowledge having received from Orangemen unequivocal
and substantial proofs of disinterested friendship and generos-
ity of heart" reads one of the bishop's observations. Because
Macdonell had been so supportive of the Conservative administration of 1836, the Orangemen cancelled their parade on 12
July, cheering him and toasting his patriotism. Observing what
seemed to be Orange esteem towards their bishop and with
the knowledge that he had served as chaplain in an occupying
regiment in Ireland, Irish Catholics were uncertain where they
stood in Macdonell's estimation.

Toronto and the Irish

What Bishop Macdonell failed to perceive was that York

was the rising commercial centre of Upper Canada and merited more concentrated ecclesiastical attention. He mistakenly believed that the Rideau Canal would make Kingston the capital of the province and, therefore, chose it as his See. Besides, Kingston was a short distance from Glengarry where Macdonell kept his major residence, among his own people. He travelled to Toronto only on business or when Council met. It was not until two years after Macdonell's death that the Church recognized the importance of Toronto and made it a separate diocese, divided from Kingston, in 1842.

Toronto was a focus for Irish Catholics. They settled on the waterfront, in Cabbage Town and in the liberties on the town's perimeters. Among that pre-famine group there arose a number of outspoken ethnic leaders like Francis Collins of the *Canadian Freeman*, and James King and Father William O'Grady of the *Correspondent and Advocate* who supported reform politics. To quell them, Bishop Macdonell threatened to excommunicate Collins for attacking the Compact, and later on did excommunicate James King and suspended Father O'Grady for stirring revolt.

As Upper Canada approached political rebellion by the 1830s, the vast diocese of Kingston was also in a state of unrest. As Bishop of Kingston, Macdonell's span of control was too large to be effective; changes were required or authority over priests and laity would be eroded.

Conflicts

Irish Catholics in the Gore district of Toronto refused to support the clergy; Macdonell responded by withdrawing the sacraments from the congregation. In Penetanguishene, the church wardens refused to pay the priest's salary, forcing him to beg among the people. Defying Macdonell's endorsement of Tory politics and his cry for loyalty, many priests looked upon William Lyon Mackenzie as the Daniel O'Connell of Upper Canada. Even in Kingston, Macdonell's own See, the Irish demanded that church land be registered in the name of the laity and not in that of an episcopal land speculator. That problem was not settled until 1845 when the Church was granted the right to act as a corporation.

Responding to what he perceived as a lack of trust among the laity, Macdonell instructed priests to say Mass at inconvenient times until the people came to their senses. Irish priests in Bytown incited the various factions in the Church to the extent that Governor Sir John Colborne directed Bishop Macdonell to replace the priests with his Vicar General, W.P. Macdonald. In Niagara, the Irish petitioned for the removal of the priest because of a diminishing congregation; only half the pews were filled and the remaining adherents refused to make up the difference in salary the priest required for survival.

With such overt statements on the part of Catholics in Kingston, Bytown, Penetanguishene, and Niagara, it was obvious that the Church was in disarray and that some decisive action was needed. Early in 1831 the bishop thought of holding a meeting of all the clergy, but there is no evidence the meeting was ever held.[6] Perhaps the ensuing events of 1831 prohibited it from taking place.

The congregation in Sandwich had become bitterly divided along political, educational, and ethnic lines. The French priests Fathers J. Crevier and Fluet were deeply involved in the disputes and were criticized by the minority English-speaking Irish and Scottish laity, as well as by some of the more conservative French. Then the parish priest, Father Crevier, was accused of disposing of £2000 New York currency. He refused to answer questions addressed to him, so Bishop Macdonell sent from York his newly appointed Vicar-General, William O'Grady, to audit the books. Crevier had falsified the records, but he surrounded himself with a group of French supporters. When O'Grady suspended Fathers Crevier and Fluet and placed the church in Sandwich under interdict, Crevier appealed over the head of Bishop Macdonell to the Bishop of

Quebec who, in return, espoused Crevier's cause. O'Grady, who by this time had returned to York, was made to look the fool. Father Fluet left the Church and became a Protestant; Crevier, without any stigma, became Bishop Macdonell's secretary at York. But Fr. O'Grady was made the scapegoat, with Bishop Macdonell denying him the editorship of *The Catholic*, which was given to the bishop's friend, W. P. Macdonald.

The events in Sandwich were but a prelude to the occurrences in York. Originally, Father O'Grady had left Ireland and travelled as chaplain with a regiment assigned to settle in Brazil. But the venture failed and O'Grady emigrated instead to York in 1828. After checking O'Grady's testimonials, Bishop Macdonell placed him at St. Paul's in charge of the Mission at York, replacing Father Angus Macdonell, the bishop's nephew. Father O'Grady achieved some success in organizing what had been a neglected mission for, according to the exemplary mission priest, Father Edward Gordon,

> *He appears to be activated by no other motive than that of advancing the interest of Holy Religion; it is truly edifying to see the number that go to the Sacraments; not only the poor (Irish) but the most respectable heads of families are frequently seen at the Holy Communion. He has commenced, a few Sundays past, a series of sermons stressing the marks of the True Church; the most part of the Protestants of York go to hear him.*[7]

Initially, Father O'Grady used Bishop Macdonell's methods to extend the influence of the Church in the Home District. His visitations covered not only the town of York but also the surrounding townships where he established Sunday schools and building committees to collect funds for churches. From Sir John Colborne he obtained in York a lot worth £1000 for a school and the promise of ten additional acres. Convinced of the importance of York, O'Grady tried to influence the bishop to make it a Catholic centre. Because Kingston was far away and St. Raphael's further, Father O'Grady asked him to reside part of the year "at York where certainly the sphere of your Lordship's utility must be considerably enlarged."[8]

In trying to create a strong Catholic laity in York, O'Grady's popularity with the Irish increased. But it declined with the Compact elite. Father O'Grady's demands for compliance with Church law in the practice of religion, his rigid opposition to membership in the Masonic Order, and the raising of sons as Protestants by prior arrangement in mixed marriages, rankled the elite Catholics, who accused him of going beyond his jurisdiction. Because O'Grady was alienating the Tory Compact group in the Church and had caused problems with the Bishop of Quebec in handling the Crevier case, Macdonell sought to remove him, even though he was held in fearfully high esteem by the Irish. The bishop found what he needed in an article published by the radical journalist Francis Collins. The latter, who had been under threat of excommunication by Bishop Macdonell for his attack on the ruling Compact elite, hated O'Grady because of a rebuke concerning the practice of his religion. In the 2 May 1833 edition of the *Canadian Freeman*, Collins cast aspersions on O'Grady's character, implying an adulterous relationship with his sister-in-law: "(O'Grady) became pompous, got a gig and a sleigh, and drove the lady who accompanied him from Rio through town and country, by night and by day, using his brother as a coachman."

That unproven and slanderous accusation caused a break between the bishop and O'Grady which ended with the suspension of the priest and the withdrawal of his assistant. The bishop placed St. Paul's Church under interdict. Thereupon some four hundred Irish followers of Father O'Grady, those of the lower order in Bishop Macdonell's estimation, seized St. Paul's Church and locked the bishop out; he had to say Mass in a building known then, in York, as the Soup Kitchen.

49

Throughout 1833-34 legal actions ensued over the possession of the church, which the Bishop finally won. The Irish collected funds and sent O'Grady to Rome, where he was ordered to submit to Macdonell's authority. During his absence a petition, signed by eight hundred Irishmen, labelled Bishop Macdonell a tyrant and a political partisan, and demanded an end to a pensioned clergy. The petition became public knowledge, having been presented to the government. It was printed in the press and from there carried to Rome.

An embarrassed Bishop Macdonell had to defend his position. He attacked his enemies publicly, declaring them unworthy of being heard. Thereupon the suspended Father O'Grady began his journalistic career in earnest together with the excommunicated James King. As joint owners of the *Correspondent*, they supported the politics of William Lyon Mackenzie against the Family Compact. O'Grady became actively involved in the reform movement and wrote the Declaration of Reformers of the City of Toronto in 1837. In the end, however, it was O'Grady who kept the Irish out of the Rebellion while Bishop Macdonell, through his powerful friends, gained the credit.[9]

To his death, Macdonell clung to the old ways that had served him well in the past but placed him beyond the reach of the people. And even in his choice of Rémigius Gaulin as Auxiliary Bishop, his judgement was questionable, for Gaulin was to suffer mental illness shortly after the succession in 1840 and was virtually ineffectual.

The authorities in Rome realized that many Catholics lived in the central portion of Upper Canada, which had been the hot bed of revolt, and decided it was essential to have a bishop in their midst whose presence might help to quell civic and religious insubordination. Michael Power, an Irish Canadian, became the first Bishop of Toronto in 1842. After two years he wrote: "I have but twenty clergymen throughout the whole country . . . I have neither colleges, nor schools, nor men."[10] Bishop Macdonell had been a great missionary prelate, but the age of missions had passed him by.

References:

1. W. J. Macdonnell, *Reminiscences of the late Hon. and Right Rev. Alexander Macdonell, first Catholic Bishop of Upper Canada* (Toronto: Williamson, 1888), pp.2-8; Kathleen Toomey, *Alexander Macdonell, the Scot Years, 1762-1804* (Toronto: Canadian Catholic Historical Assoc., 1985), pp.40-97.

2. *Reminiscences*, p.7.

3. J. A. Macdonell, *A sketch of the life of the Hon. and Rt. Rev. Alexander Macdonell* (Office of the Glengarrian and Alexandria, 1890), p.147.

4. J. E. Ray, *Bishop Alexander Macdonell and the politics of Upper Canada* (Toronto: Ontario Historical Society, 1974), in general.

5. Archives of Ontario (hereafter AO), Macdonell papers, A. Macdonell to Bishop McEachern, 3 April 1829.

6. Murray W. Nicolson, *The Catholic Church and the Irish in Victorian Toronto*. PhD diss. (University of Guelph, 1981), pp.49-91.

7. Archives of the Roman Catholic Archdiocese of Toronto (hereafter Arcat), Macdonell papers, E. Gordon to Bishop Macdonell, 11 March 1830.

8. AO, Macdonell papers, O'Grady to Macdonell, 16 November 1829.

9. M. W. Nicolson "William O'Grady and the Catholic Church in Toronto prior to the Irish Famine", in Mark McGowan and Brian Clarke, eds., *Catholics at the "Gathering Place"* (Toronto: Canadian Catholic Historical Association, 1993), pp.23-37.

10. Arcat, Power papers, Power to Bishop Kinsella, 8 July 1844.

CHAPTER FIVE

BISHOP MICHAEL POWER

A martyr to duty

Michael Power

Following the 1837 Rebellion, the need to break up the vast Diocese of Kingston was recognized by both Church and state. Father Michael Power, recognized for his wisdom, firmness, and piety, was the unanimous choice of the Canadian bishops to become the first bishop of Toronto. Believing himself unworthy of the task, Power still obeyed his superiors. His potential was not fully realized, however, because his tenure was too short—just five years. On October 23, 1847, *The Cross*, a Catholic newspaper published in Halifax, reported that a native son, Dr. Michael Power, had succumbed to typhus. With the eloquence of the age, the obituary read:

> *He fell a martyr to duty —concluding, as he commenced, his sacerdotal services in the church by acts of spiritual heroism and self-devotion. From the Acolyte at the altar of the old wooden fabric of St. Peter's, in this his native city, till his attainment of the episcopal dignity at Toronto, this writer has had opportunities of observing the course of the deceased Prelate, and deeply deplores the inefficiency of his pen, to depict it as it merits.*

Born in Halifax, Nova Scotia, in 1804, where his parents had settled after emigrating from Waterford, Ireland, Power attended St. Peter's Church. In the absence of Catholic schools, he attended a local grammar school and was taught Latin by his pastor, Father E. Burke (who later became Vicar Apostolic of Nova Scotia) and by Father Mignault, a Sulpician. Afterwards he was sent to the

Seminary of St. Sulpice in Montreal, then to the Seminary of Quebec. He was ordained at Montreal by Bishop Dubois of New York in 1827.

Following pastoral ministries at Drummondville, at Montebello, and at the Catholic missions on both sides of the Ottawa River, he was appointed pastor at Laprairie and Vicar-General of the Diocese of Montreal in 1839. In 1841, Alexander Macdonell's successor to the Diocese of Kingston, Bishop Rémigius Gaulin, was in poor physical and mental health and was seeking a coadjutor. He appealed to the Holy See and, learning of Father Power's abilities, submitted his name for consideration. At the same time, Gaulin applied to Rome and to the British government for a division of his vast diocese. Because the province was becoming increasingly Irish, he proposed to Bishop Ignace Bourget of Montreal that Montreal's Vicar-General Power was a candidate acceptable to both Rome and London: "He is sufficiently Irish to be well thought of here and sufficiently Canadian to live up to all expectations."[1]

Pope Gregory XVI agreed to the division, and Bishop Bourget and Father Power went to London to obtain assent from the British government for the proposed arrangements. Power had the foresight to explain the value of episcopal supervision over unruly citizens:

> A Catholic bishop in case of emergency will provide more authority over those committed to his care than an ordinary clergyman, his presence and his advice may also prove highly serviceable to Her Majesty's government in quelling that spirit of insubordination and fierce democratic spirit which unhappily exists to a formidable degree in many parts of the frontier line.[2]

Desiring the continued loyalty of her Catholic subjects, the British government welcomed the plan to divide the Kingston diocese. On December 17, 1841, Pope Gregory issued a Bull severing from the diocese of Kingston all

St. Paul's Church

parts of Upper Canada that lay west of the district of Newcastle and naming Michael Power first bishop of the new diocese. Power was consecrated bishop in 1842 in Laprairie, Québec, by Bishop Gaulin, assisted by Bishops Turgeon and Bourget.

Organizing a new diocese

Bishop Power faced an enormous task in trying to fulfil the spiritual needs of his subjects. The lack of qualified priests was a pressing problem. Acknowledging the void, he admitted to Bishop Kinsella of Ireland in 1842 that "I am determined to have a whole district without any spiritual assistance rather than to confide the poor people into the hands of improper or suspended men."[3]

Soon after Bishop Power took possession of his See, he called the clergy to a five-day spiritual retreat, followed by a synod at St. Paul's Church in Toronto. In an impressive ceremony, he consecrated the Diocese of Toronto to the Sacred Heart of Jesus. He then drew up statutes for governing the diocese, and announced that a seminary college was a prerequisite to educate native Canadian priests to serve the needs of the growing population. Additionally, he stated his desire to establish a college at Sandwich to be a centre for the Indian Missions in Upper Canada, under the direction of the Jesuit Fathers, thereby allowing them to renew their work among the Indians.

The purpose of the regulations adopted at that first synod was to improve discipline among the clergy and laity. Priests were not permitted to wander beyond the limits of their parish; they were to reside in it and were to obtain the bishop's permission for an absence of more than a week. They were to dress in the cassock and avoid any intimate association with women. Confessional boxes were to be constructed in all churches so that sins would not become common knowledge among the people. Private confession outside the church was forbidden, except in cases where the parishioner was sick or deaf. No fee was to be charged for the administration of a sacrament. Baptismal fonts were to be installed in all churches. Private baptism in the home of a parishioner was not permitted except when a child was in danger of death. Parental consent was required for the baptism of a child. No marriages were to take place in homes, and newly arrived immigrants had to produce evidence of their right to marry. By January 1, 1843, all priests were to have set up a ledger in which they recorded all baptisms, confirmations, marriages and burials. The use of the Roman Missal and Breviary, and Butler's *Catechism,* was to be the norm.

Bishop Power travelled extensively, visiting Amherstburg, Sandwich, and Tilbury, and going as far north as Manitoulin Island. He addressed the clergy and laity on the value of charity and good works, and on the education and training of children. One need he recognized was for the establishment of the Association for the Propagation of the Faith, which he described as "one of the most admirable institutions and greatest works of modern times." The words in his pastoral letter of 21 February 1844 are as applicable today as they were then:

> *We should not forget that we have not ful-*
> *filled our duty towards our neighbour if we con-*
> *fine our charity and our solicitude to those with*
> *whom we live; for the divine light of our revela-*
> *tion shows us a brother, a friend in being a mem-*
> *ber of the human race ... that all men, without*
> *exception, are our neighbours and should be*
> *dear to us.*

From his diocesan travels, Bishop Power discerned the need for decentralization. He created six deaneries, covering all of Southern Ontario up to the borders of Lake Huron and Lake Superior. In some of the more distant areas, the rural dean was also vicar forane, a position which carried additional authority and independence.

In 1844, Bishop Power joined with other bishops in Upper and Lower Canada to successfully petition the Pope for the creation of an ecclesiastical province in Canada. The dioceses of Quebec, Montreal, Kingston, and Toronto were thus united under the metropolitan Province of Quebec, which became an Archdiocese. In a pastoral letter to his laity, Bishop Power expressed his expectations thus:

> *Let us pray that this complete Ecclesiastical*
> *organization may tend to the more rapid*
> *progress of the Catholic church, afford to her*
> *now well established hierarchy the means of*
> *labouring together in more perfect unity and*
> *design, and by the united efforts of her first pas-*
> *tors, of infusing new vigour and fresh energy to*
> *the most remote and more infant portions of the*
> *Catholic Church in this province.*[4]

Let us recall that the Canadian bishops had achieved a major feat, one that, as yet, had not been granted in Great Britain, where a Catholic hierarchy was not restored until 1850. Dr. Wiseman of England (later Cardinal) sent his congratulations: "You, on your side, have experienced the blessing of a properly constituted ecclesiastical government, sufficiently to understand our eagerness to obtain the same privilege."[5]

St. Michael's Cathedral

Building a Cathedral

During these ecclesiastical and government negotiations, Bishop Power also decided that he needed a central focus for his own diocese: a cathedral and a bishop's "palace". St. Paul's Church, built in the early 1820s in the midst of Irish settlement on the west side of the Don River, was the only Catholic church in Toronto and served as a cathedral when the diocese was formed. But it was an age of cathedral building, and Bishop Power was aware that similar projects had been undertaken in Kingston, Philadelphia, Chicago, Mobile, and Louisville. He purchased land in an area that had not yet been incorporated into the city. He asked for a general subscription from the public, Catholics and Protestants alike, and for a contribution of five shillings from each Catholic worker. Excavation for St. Michael's Cathedral began in a spirit of cooperation on April 7, 1845:

> An ox was roasted whole, to cheer the parish volunteers digging under the direction of John Harper, contractor for the masonry, brickwork and carpentry. Ishmael Iredale was engaged to roof the building, and John Craig bespoken for the painting. Craig assigned the window sashes to the painstaking care of his young apprentice, Michael O'Connor, the only Roman Catholic in his employ. [6]

The Cathedral was not dedicated until September 29, 1848, a year after Power's death. The structure was encumbered with a huge debt, partially due to the impact of the Irish Famine on the diocese. Catholic laymen, John Elmsley and S.G. Lynn, guaranteed the debt, and Power's succcessor, Bishop Armand de Charbonnel, lifted it entirely.

More Irish were coming

When Power proceeded with his financially draining plan of cathedral building, he could not forecast the impact of the Irish Famine on his diocese. Because he had such a versatile mind, one can only wonder at what might have been, had Power's tenure extended beyond five years.

Power was quick to notice that the Irish made up the bulk of his flock: "My diocese is mostly inhabited by Irishmen dispersed over an immense tract of land, bounded on all sides by the Great Lakes. Every day our steamer boats bring in new reinforcements from the mother country."[7]

Having been left a meagre inheritance of twenty clergy and numerous complaints from a laity who had suffered at the hands of unsupervised and unscrupulous priests, Power tried to acquire men from Ireland to serve this ever-growing group of Irish immigrants. He anticipated a rewarding life for "young, well disposed, efficient clergymen", who would "always have food and raiment". But, aware of the effects of loneliness and isolation, he admitted that "for a time they may have to contend with those difficulties which are inseparable from the settlement of a new country."[8]

Power was a conscientious taskmaster. Having set his standards at that first synod, he expected compliance. Moreover, having explained to the British government the value of a bishop's authority, he would not tolerate behaviour among his faithful that might jeopardize the Catholic position in the civil realm. As an example, Father W. P. McDonagh in St. Catharines reported faction fighting among the Irish canal workers there. He attributed it to secret societies which were common in the 1840s throughout Upper Canada, particularly in areas of canal building. They were an outcropping of organizations that had arisen in Ireland. The Bishop advised Father McDonagh to adopt any means to suppress them. So Father McDonagh walked between the lines of the warring Cork and Connaught men, holding a Host and chalice in his hands, an act which quelled the violence and received the approbation of his Bishop:

> You can let the people know that henceforth it will be a case reserved to me and that I am disposed to employ the fervor of censures of the Church for suppression of these illegal societies. I feel as Catholics and Irishmen they will possess sufficient religion, honour, and respect for themselves not to compel me, in the presence of a Protestant community, to denounce them as dupes of wicked, designing men and refractory members of the Church. [9]

The clergy were also expected to be obedient to rules, and infractions were countered with disciplinary measures. Although there was no dissenting voice at the first synod, some priests were resistant to wearing the soutane because it marked them as easy targets for abuse from members of the Orange Order. When Bishop Power learned that Father W.P. Macdonald, vicar-general, appeared publicly without the soutane, he suspended him from his position, leaving him as parish priest in Hamilton. Yet Power usually relented when the priest in question complied with his directives, as did Macdonald, who then was returned to office.

Bishop Power was also required to deal with the school issue in a period when new political forces were at work in the Union of the Canadas. He lacked the strong political influence wielded by Bishop Alexander Macdonell in the colonial administration and, therefore, had to tread cautiously to avoid offence. There is no evidence during his episcopacy of the extreme ethno-religious hatred that was to explode later, no doubt the consequence of the massive immigration of Famine Irish.

Harmony over schools

The School Act of 1846 included the religious clauses of the 1843 Act under which the Board of Education was to be composed of clerical and lay representatives from the six major denominations. Bishop Power was well regarded and, therefore, was selected for the chairmanship of the Board of Education for Upper Canada. Although he might not have perceived the extent to which the public school system was to become a Protestant institution, Power's acceptance of the chairmanship through association could be viewed as a controversial act. Historian Franklin Walker believes that the bishop took the position to "demonstrate his desire to associate himself with the new education movement."[10] This association does not necessarily imply that he didn't support separate schools. In fact, Power very much believed that parents had a grave responsibility to provide a Catholic education for their children.

Whatever the reason, Egerton Ryerson, the Methodist bishop and leader of the Protestant majority, used the bishop's apparent willingness to cooperate like a stick to beat against his successor's inflexibility on the separate school issue. When Power died, Egerton Ryerson was "astounded and deeply affected" by the death of this "exceedingly agreeable and amiable man" who had chaired the Board of Education "with firmness ... zeal and intelligence" and a "scrupulous regard ... for the views and rights and wishes of Protestants."[11]

However, the fight for separate schools did not begin in earnest until several years after Power's death when Ryerson had to face Bishop de Charbonnel, a determined and more direct, less diplomatic individual.

Religious orders needed

What Bishop Power did discern for education was a need to bring religious orders into the diocese. He wrote the General of the Society of Jesus in 1842 and through him obtained priests for the Parish of the Assumption at Sandwich (modern-day Windsor). The Jesuits also arrived in 1846 at Penetanguishene, where they began to plan for the religious education of the Indians in the Upper Great Lakes. In 1847 Power asked the Christian Brothers to take over elementary schools of the diocese, but that request was not fulfilled until 1850.

In January of 1847, the bishop travelled to Europe in search of priests and funds to relieve the debt of the Cathedral. He had a full agenda. In Ireland, he arranged for the services of the Sisters of the Institute of the Blessed Virgin Mary (Loretto Sisters, IBVM) with the expectation that

> the Day School will, I hope, be numerously attended after a few weeks, and the Common School in great numbers ...The people, Catholics, mostly Irish or of Irish descent, are not rich. Some families are well able to educate their daughters, but many Protestants will feel happy in being able to avail themselves of the opportunity of giving their daughters a good, sound education.[12]

Power's negotiations with the Sisters took several weeks, during which time he witnessed the distress of the peasantry in Ireland. Ironically, his association with the Sisters was shortlived, for their arrival in Toronto coincided with Power's death.

While in England, Power discussed with Lord Grey the persecution of one of his missionaries by agents of the Indian Department. He proceeded to Paris and made arrangements for the future welfare of the German settlers in his diocese. After that, he went to Rome.

By the time he returned to Toronto, the Famine was emptying Ireland and its effects were being felt in the new world. From Grosse Ile, near Quebec City, to Toronto, death from typhus was a common occurrence among the debilitated immigrants.

As Fr. J.R. Teefy, C.S.B., editor of the 1892 *Archdiocese of Toronto Jubilee Volume* , records, in all, 90,150 emigrants landed at Quebec in 1847:

> There had died on the voyage 5,282 and in quarantine 3,389, a total of nearly nine thousand victims to long years of government and oppression in holy yet unhappy Ireland... Those who passed the inspection of the quarantine officers and were allowed to proceed up the river to Montreal and to Upper Canada, carried with them the seeds of the pestilence and scattered them far and wide. The fever broke out simultaneously in many places and added victims by the hundreds to the already vast total on board ship and at Grosse Ile. Over seven hundred died at Quebec; 3,330 at Lachine, and 3,048 at various points in Ontario, not including Toronto. Eight hundred and sixty-three died and were buried in long trenches near St. Paul's Church. While the city hid in fear of the contagion, Bishop Power gathered what help he could to tend the plague-stricken and starving Irish immigrants. Archdeacon Hay, himself ill with tuberculosis, Father Dirwan, Father Proulx from the north, Father Sanderl from Waterloo, Father Schneider from

*Goderich, and Father Quinlan from Brantford
answered their bishop's plea. These men, along
with John Elmsley, a dedicted Catholic layman, and
the Anglican Bishop John Strachan, courageously
entered the fever sheds set up on the wharves to
tend the sick and the dying.*

Fr. Teefy further writes:

> *One by one they sank under the work from sheer
> fatigue, or themselves succumbed to the fever; the
> Bishop was then left almost alone, to battle as best he
> could with the difficulties of the situation... Then
> came a call at midnight that a poor woman lay dying
> at the immigrant sheds, and asked for succour. There
> being no one else to answer to the call, the Bishop
> recognizing in the poorest and most helpless of the
> Irish immigrants a member of his flock, placed the
> Bread of Life in his bosom and went out into the
> night to fortify a soul for its last journey. He fulfilled
> his mission, but, as it proved, at the cost of his own
> precious life. Bishop Power contracted the disease
> and succumbed on October 1, 1847.*

In Halifax, the town of Power's birth, the sentiments of
many were echoed by the Catholic newspaper, *The Cross,*
on 23 October 1847:

> *The loss to the Diocese of Toronto which Dr.
> Power distinguished by the value of his sacred
> offices, and the virtues of his life —is at this
> moment heavy and severe. It is said that neither
> night nor day witnessed his absence from the
> depositaries of the diocese, until at length kneel-
> ing over the bed of infection, and listening to the
> sorrows of some poor penitent, he inhaled the
> miasma of death. Grief of such a loss is natural.
> The associates of his youth, who well remember
> him, deeply lament in this community the priva-
> tion Canada has sustained.*

References:

1. Archives, Archdiocese of Montreal, Kingston section, R. Gaulin to I.
Bourget, 25 April 1841.
2. *Arcat, Power papers, Power to Lord Stanley, 27 Sept. 1841.*

3. *Ibid.*, Power to Bishop Kinsella, 8 July 1842.

4. *Ibid.*, Pastoral address, 29 Dec. 1844.

5. *Ibid.*, Nicholas Cardinal Wiseman to Rt. Rev. bishops of Canada, undated.

6. Marion MacRae, Anthony Adamson, *Hallowed walls: church archi-tecture of Upper Canada* (Toronto: Clarke, Irwin, 1975), p.148.

7. Arcat, *Power papers*, Power to Bishop Kinsella, 8 July 1842.

8. *Ibid.*

9. *Ibid.*, Power to W. P. McDonagh, 10 March, 1844.

10. F. Walker, *Catholic education and politics in Upper Canada* (Toronto: Dent, 1955), p.55.

11. J. Moir, *The Church in the British era* (Toronto, McGraw-Hill Ryerson, 1972), p.174.

12. M. Margorita," Institute of the Blessed Virgin Mary, Report" (Canadian Catholic Historical Association 1944-1945), pp.69-81.

CHAPTER SIX

QUEBEC AND THE WIDER EFFECTS OF THE IRISH FAMINE, 1846 to 1848

English-speaking colonists who arrived in Lower Canada (Quebec) after the Conquest, or as United Empire Loyalists following the American Revolution, were primarily Anglican. Most were merchants or professional people. Some took up farming in the Eastern Townships and a few could be found amongst the French in the areas of seigniorial tenure. Others were in the military or held administrative posts. Their prosperity was ensured, as the colonial government favoured them over the French in the distribution of positions, pensions, and contracts. For all their influence and power, however, English speakers remained a small minority, and Catholics among them were an insignificant number. Competition for jobs intensified the French-Canadian dislike of all English speakers, regardless of whether they were Protestant or Catholic.

The U.S. invasion

After the Conquest, Montreal became a British garrison and the seat of the colonial governor. It also became an important target in the eyes of American revolutionists who hoped to make Canada a fourteenth state. In fact, Montreal fell to the Americans for a brief period late in 1775, and Benjamin Franklin was dispatched to Canada during the spring of 1776 to persuade French Canadians to support the American Revolution. Included among Franklin's commissioners was Father John Carroll, a Jesuit fluent in French, appointed by the Congress to influence Montreal's Roman Catholic clergy to side with the revolutionary cause. The French clergy argued, however, that, by the Quebec Act of 1774, the British government guaranteed them rights and privileges denied Roman Catholics in the American colonies.

Franklin's mission, like the armed intervention, failed. The unpaid, unruly, occupying American troops robbed the Montrealers. Brigadier-General David Wooster, taking charge of Montreal in the name of Congress, persecuted Catholics, intimidated the clergy, and exiled prominent Tories, providing a negative example of the so-called benefits of "liberty". Nonetheless, because of Franklin's association with Father Carroll in the Montreal Mission, he recommended the latter to the Pope and, in 1789, Father Carroll became the first Catholic bishop in the United States—the Bishop of Baltimore.

The Scots

One English-speaking group that had a strong impact on the development of Montreal was the Scots, a commercially-minded people, mostly Protestant. The initial introduction of the Scots into Quebec began as captive soldiers in the war between New France and the British colonies; many of them stayed after the Conquest. They were joined by soldiers and officers of the Fraser Highlanders and the Black Watch who settled in the lower province. Immigrants from the Catholic Highland clans, particularly the Macdonnells, settled in Glengarry, in Upper Canada, where they became influential in the military and the government. They were especially instrumental in the fur trade, organizing the Hudson Bay Company and the North West Company. Consequently their time was divided between Montreal and York. The Glengarry Scots sent their sons to be educated in Montreal but, unlike the Protestant Scots, they avoided the Quebec political scene.[1]

The Irish

The Irish presence in Quebec preceded the British Conquest. According to Irish folk history, Saint Brendan came to Canada in 545 and sailed up the St. Lawrence

66

River. There is another story that the Irish penetrated the St. Lawrence Valley between 875 and 900 A.D. Several thousand Irish, English- or Gaelic-speakers, served in the French Army during the 18th Century, and many of them were garrisoned at Quebec. In 1755, an entire Irish brigade landed at Quebec and was subsequently stationed at Montreal. Some obtained seigniorial grants, others engaged in the fur trade, lumber industry, and agriculture. Thus a settlement of Irish Catholics was established in advance of General Wolfe's arrival in 1759.

Intermarriage with French Catholics hastened the absorption of the Irish, as did the practice of Irish priests gallicizing their names. Of the 2,500 families in Quebec in 1700, 100 came from Ireland and, in thirty other cases, either the husband or wife had been born in Ireland. Montreal's population in 1825 was 25,000, of whom 3,000 were Irish, and the population of Quebec City in 1830 was 32,000, with 7,000 being Irish. Both cities had a Saint Patrick's Church served by Irish priests sent out from Ireland.

Although the Irish were scattered throughout both cities, the immigrant sheds in Montreal were occupied completely by Irish, and Irish predominated in the environs of the Lachine Canal and for several blocks north. The area had the poorest housing and the lowest per capita income in the city. On the waterfront strip in Quebec, below the Plains of Abraham and west of Lower Town, Irish made up fifty per cent of the population. Many were employed in the lumber trade, having arrived from Ireland as ballast in the holds of ships which then returned to Europe with lumber.

Education was a privilege, limited to one or two years for most French and Irish children. In 1846, the Irish Catholics in Montreal were able to establish their own elementary school within the newly formed Montreal Catholic School Commission. The De La Salle Brothers held classes in 1848 for English Catholics in their Upper

Town School in Quebec City, and, in 1849, an English school was opened in Diamond Harbour, Lower Town, where many Irish Catholics lived.[2]

The "Famine Irish" and disease

Between 1832 and 1860, Quebec City was British North America's main port of entry, receiving an average of 30,000 immigrants a year, 52 percent of whom were Irish. Contagious diseases were widespread in the British Isles and brought to North America by contaminated immigrants in this period. Cholera, for example, carried to Great Britain by British soldiers returning from India, was transported to Quebec on emigrant ships with a deadly impact in 1832, killing 1,900 persons in Montreal and twice that number in Quebec City. Grosse Ile , an island thirty miles downstream from Quebec City, was set up with haste as the Quebec City quarantine station to deal with more than 100,000 immigrants in the 1832 cholera epidemic.

Typhus accompanied the Irish to Quebec City during the 1820s, when they emigrated from Ireland because of overpopulation and the re-allocation of land by the landlords. The period of greatest catastrophe, however, was 1846-1848, when many thousands were dying because of the Potato Famine in Ireland, while Britain allowed 17 million pounds' sterling worth of grain, cattle, pigs, flour, eggs and poultry to be shipped out of Ireland to England. The starving people were shipped to the New World, and the conditions under which they travelled were conducive to typhus. Of the 90,000 Irish immigrants arriving in 1847 in the port of Quebec City, typhus killed 10,000 in Canada, while another 5,000 perished in the crossing. Typhus was called variously "ship fever," "hospital fever", or "jail fever," and was defined as "essentially a fever of the poor, ill-fed, and badly housed."[3]

The number of infected Irish immigrants arriving in 1847 far surpassed the isolation and quarantine facilities of Grosse Ile. Nearby, Quebec City, exposed to the typhus epidemic, escaped relatively unscathed compared to Montreal. Twenty-two fever sheds were constructed in 1847 on the wharves at Montreal to isolate the affected, with coffins of different sizes stacked between the sheds, in a summer of intense heat. As the disease penetrated the city, panic arose, precipitating a strong anti-Irish sentiment.

Fever in Montreal

Scenes in the Montreal fever sheds were like hell on earth. The stench was overwhelming; the sick were heaped together, with corpses among them. Children could be counted in the hundreds; infants were taken from the breasts of dead mothers and youngsters shrieked for parents who had perished. Religious, clergy, and lay people of all denominations worked with the medical men to look after the sick, many of them paying with their lives later. The Grey Nuns received permission from the emigrant agent and began to nurse the sick in the sheds on June 18, 1847, and, by the 24th, two of their Sisters were stricken. More fell ill on a daily basis, until thirty of their forty professed nuns were close to death. The place was taken over by the Sisters of Providence and then by those from Hôtel Dieu who had received permission to leave their cloister to work, until the Grey Nuns once again resumed responsibility in September.

At great risk were priests who heard the confessions of the dying. At least nine English-speaking priests died in Montreal that summer and replacements came from the Jesuits at Fordham in New York. The first Rector of Trinity Anglican Church, Reverend Mark Willoughby, succumbed, along with some of his congregation, who worked among the Catholic Irish in the sheds. John Easton Mills, an American from Massachusetts who had made a fortune in the fur trade, was the mayor of Montreal. In his capacity as president of the Immigration Commission, he ordered the building of the sheds at Pointe St. Charles. Angry Montrealers threatened to toss the fever sheds into the river as more sick Irish arrived, particularly a ship containing the tenants from the Irish estates of Lord Palmerston, the British Foreign Secretary. The bilingual Mayor Mills restrained the citizens and voluntarily entered the sheds to nurse the sick, dying as a result of the contact.

Many of the orphans were cared for by the Grey Nuns in St. Patrick's Orphan Asylum of Montreal, opened in 1846. Bishop Ignace Bourget appealed to the country people to provide homes for the orphans, and the French families from surrounding parishes each adopted one or two of the unfortunate children.[4]

Three monuments

Workmen digging the approaches to the Victoria Bridge in 1859 unearthed the bones of typhus victims. They erected a simple but impressive monument, a large boulder taken from the river bed. Known as the "Irish Stone," it was enscribed as a tribute by the workmen: "To Preserve From Desecration The Remains of 6000 Immigrants Who Died of Ship Fever, A.D. 1847-48."[5]

In acknowledgement of the 1847 epidemic, a four-sided monument, on the site of what had been the immigrant cemetery, commemorates the dead: "In this secluded spot lie the mortal remains of 5,294 persons, who, flying from pestilence and famine in the year 1847, found in America but a grave."[6] It was erected by Dr. Douglas, the medical officer in charge of the quarantine station, and eighteen medical assistants on duty on Grosse Ile that year. A second monument at Grosse Ile, a Celtic cross of granite, was erected by the Ancient Order of Hibernians in America in 1909. Its inscription in English, Irish, and French also pays tribute to the Irish immigrants who perished there in 1847.

The plight of the survivors

Survival for the Irish was difficult. Already feeble, emaciated and poor, they had to face the bitter Canadian winter reliant upon the charity of the urban centres and the Church. Untrained, uneducated, they worked at whatever job they could find. Crowded into multiple dwellings, they kept pigs and chickens in the kitchen, saving the manure to plant patches of potatoes and cabbage in the spring. What sustained them were their culture and social habits of drinking, fighting, wild weddings and wakes. They survived to become part of the English-speaking Catholic population of Quebec. Those in the townships who initially retained their ethnic identity were soon absorbed, or left as the French took over their churches and the area.

At the time of the conquest, Great Britain was considerate of the terms that protected the religious rights of French Canadians. On the other hand, it treated the Catholic Highland Scots and the Irish in a despicable manner, denying them religious rights and creating unbearable social conditions. As English-speaking Catholics, the Irish particularly were ostracized in the United Canadas because of their religion by those who spoke the common language, and by their French co-religionists because of their different language. Hugh MacLennan, a Canadian novelist, coined the phrase "two solitudes" to describe the co-existence of French and English-speaking communities on the same territory while leading parallel, but isolated, lives. The Irish, in the words of the historian John Moir, were "a third solitude in the Canadian milieu."

References:

1. Henry B. Best, "The auld alliance in New France", and Elaine A. Mitchell, "The Scot in the fur trade", in W. Stanford Reid, *The Scottish tradition in Canada* (Toronto: McClelland and Stewart, 1977), pp.15-25; 27-47.

2. Marianna O'Gallagher, "The Irish in Quebec", and D. Aidan

McQuillan, "Beaurivage: the development of an Irish ethnic identity in rural Quebec, 1820-1860", in *The untold story of the Irish in Canada,* v.1, pp.253-261; 263-270.

3. M. O'Gallagher, Grosse Ile: gateway to Canada ,1832-1937 (Quebec: Carraig Books, 1984), pp.1; 19-26; 50-53; *Grosse Ile, National historic site* (Ottawa: Environment Canada Parks Service, 1992), pp.9-11.

4. E. A. Collard, *Montreal: the days that are no more* (Toronto: Totem Books, 1976), pp.122-129.

5. Ibid., p.121.

6. *Grosse Ile, National historic site*, p.88.

CHAPTER SEVEN

THE BEGGAR BISHOP
Armand de Charbonnel

U nlike the situation in Lower Canada, Catholics were a small minority of the total population in Upper Canada. The Catholic Scots in Glengarry and the French in the Windsor and Penetanguishene areas were greatly outnumbered by the Irish, who settled primarily in the central area of the province. By mid-nineteenth century, Upper Canada was moving from a colonial economy towards an industrial one. Indian trails were replaced by roads into the Canadian Shield and to Georgian Bay. By the 1850s surveyors had laid out farm lots as well as roads, and settlements expanded. Mills were congregating points for the scattered farmers, as were the blacksmith shops, general stores, and churches of the villages and emerging towns. Railways opened up the area, and the Grand Trunk which linked Montreal to Toronto in 1856 promoted economic advancement.

In this environment, Catholics were on the outside looking in—economically, socially and politically. Their identity as Irish had ostracized them because of their religion and because of the contagion they brought with them during periods of high immigration. Certainly their numbers grew after the Famine migration in 1847. They were fewer than 3,000 in Toronto in 1835, but 7,940 by 1851. Toronto's streets, like those in Kingston, Montreal, and Quebec, were crowded with emaciated, destitute Irish immigrants in the summer of 1847, many with typhus. On August 16, the Toronto hospital was crammed with 872 patients when it could only hold about 150. St. Paul's Cemetery on Power Street was filled to overflowing. Moreover, the immigrants who moved to surrounding towns and farming communities carried the disease with them.

73

The poor Famine Irish immigrants enlarged the slum area of Toronto. They were congregated in an area from Queen Street to the waterfront, and from Parliament Street east to the Don Basin and the liberties beyond. This area was known as Cabbage Town, and sometimes called Irish Town or Slab Town. The Church introduced religious orders and established social agencies to assist the deprived Irish in their transition as Catholics in a new, hostile environment.

The growth of Catholic institutions and churches put fear into the predominantly Protestant majority, who saw this as the infiltration of 'popery' into their province. At issue, particularly, was the push for separate schools which promoted a backlash. Both the Tory and Reform parties upheld anti-Catholic sentiment at times. The Orange Order, initially an Irish Protestant organization, expanded to become a powerful Protestant association that controlled the public schools, the militia, the police, and the civic administration, shutting the Irish out of municipal employment. Moreover, it fostered movements like the Equal Rights and the Protestant Protective Association with their overtly anti-Catholic platforms.

As we have seen then, the famine in Ireland had an enormous effect on the development of the Catholic Church in Upper Canada. Places like Toronto were hard pressed to deal with Irish immigrants, most of them Catholic, who arrived in a state of destitution. The city's charitable resources were stretched to the limit, and the Church's were non-existent. The untimely death of Bishop Power in 1847 added to the crisis, and Toronto was left without a bishop for three years.[1]

The benevolence of a layman: John Elmsley

During the interregnum, two influential laymen, John Elmsley and S.G. Lynn, both converts to Catholicism, helped to maintain the financial integrity of the diocese by personally guaranteeing the debts on Power's estate and on

St. Michael's Cathedral. Ironically, Elmsley, first considered by the Irish as a pompous, meddling Tory squire, gained the respect of the famine immigrants for his dedication to them:

> Amidst the ridicule of his former friends, some of whom abandoned him, he went about doing good. His care of the poor, of the widows and orphans who were swept away by the fever, was incessant . . . . He nursed and tended the sick; he consoled the dying; he buried the victims of the terrible scourge; he washed with his own hands the poor bereaved orphans whose condition would have excited disgust in the minds of those who lay claim to no ordinary share of humanity and benevolence.[2]

He is commemorated in Elmsley Place and Elmsley Hall at St. Michael's College.

While Elmsley used his own and the Church's money (such as the Offertory fund) in aid of the poor, he dispensed it from City Hall, thus motivating the civic authorities to increase their own financial help. He also served on the board of the House of Industry, a secular institution which housed the poor. In 1853, however, he resigned, when it was reported that the House was using proselytizing tactics to turn Catholics away from their religion by way of offering soup.

In 1849, Elmsley and his wife organized the Catholic Ladies of Toronto, to counteract the Committee of the Widows and Orphans Fund, through which Irish Catholic children were being given to Protestant families. The Elmsleys obtained a property on Nelson Street which became a Catholic orphanage, with the Catholic Ladies supplying bedding, clothing and cooking necessities, and others donating food and fuel. Servant girls, under the direction of a matron, cared for the children while awaiting job opportunities.

The new bishop

Armand de Charbonnel

Armand François-Marie, Comte de Charbonnel, was born of privileged parents in Southern France on December 1, 1802. He was educated by a group of diocesan priests known as Basilians from the parish of that name; they were the founders of the Congregation of St. Basil. Despite his father's wish that he enter the military, Charbonnel went to the Sulpician Seminary at Issy and was ordained a priest in 1825. For fifteen years he taught dogma and Scripture at various Sulpician seminaries in France, but much of his priestly career was spent in avoiding opportunities of promotion. During riots in Lyons in 1834, he was instrumental in saving the city from pillage, and was offered the Cross of the Legion of Honour by King Louis Philippe—which he declined. To escape being made a bishop, he volunteered as a missionary to Canada.

Father Charbonnel worked among the Irish in Montreal from 1840 to 1847. During that time, Archbishop Blanc of New Orleans sought him as coadjutor, and Governor-General Sydenham also pressed him to accept a bishopric. But he replied to the latter, "If I wanted to be a bishop, I would not have left France." Like Bishop Power, he fell ill with typhus contracted from the famine immigrants. He was recalled to France to convalesce, and then became Professor of Theology in the Seminary at Aix-en-Provence. But when the Canadian hierarchy pleaded with the Vatican to appoint him to the See of Toronto, all his protests were of no avail; Pope Pius IX personally bestowed the episcopal dignity on him on May 26, 1850.[3]

Arrival in Toronto

One of Bishop Charbonnel's first undertakings was to address the laity in St. Michael's Cathedral on "The Duties of the Good Shepherd." On October 30, 1850, The Mirror reported:

> He began by hoping that they would excuse his imperfect English . . . He spoke of his labours in Montreal amongst the Irish immigrants . . . . He stood then before them as their chief Pastor, ready at all times to risk everything to sacrifice everything, even life itself, if necessary, for the welfare of the flock committed to his care. In proof of his entire devotion to their services he assured them that he had made over the whole of his paternal estate in France to assist in liquidating the debt contracted for the building of the magnificent Cathedral in which they were, and for such other religious purposes as the Diocese mostly stood in need of, without so much as reserving a farthing for his own private use. He concluded by promising to visit them all; but he wanted especially to see the poor, to cheer, to console, and if possible to relieve them.

With such dedication, Charbonnel applied himself to his enormous task. He realized at once the need to provide assistance for the poor, the sick, hungry, and unskilled immigrants if they were to survive. He soon invited from France religious orders which had profited from the devotional, moral, and social renewal of St. Alphonsus de Liguori. Through them, he planned to establish schools and seminaries and to serve the neglected spiritual needs of the laity. To begin with, he had only two churches, two priests, and a few Sisters of Loretto in Toronto, and twenty-eight priests scattered throughout his diocese.

Charbonnel established a Cathedral Loan Fund to reduce the debt on the unfinished building. Money flowed in from Canada East, Canada West, and the United States. Catholics from Montreal, where Charbonnel had never accepted a stipend, helped him with land and savings and insurance policies. He also established a Toronto Savings Bank to keep track of money loaned to the Church, and to encourage the laity to save for education, housing, times of illness or unemployment, or old age. In all financial matters, Charbonnel required strict accountability. Each parish or institution was to keep its books up-to-date, and priests were to keep accurate records of all collections and other income (including bazaars and picnics) so that the diocese could receive its Cathedraticum of one-tenth of parish revenue. None of this money went to keep Charbonnel in the style of a count or a bishop; in his personal habits, food, and clothing, he adopted the lifestyle of a beggar, and he expected a similar charitable commitment from his clergy.

In 1852 the Bishop made a visitation throughout his vast diocese—all of southern Ontario. Subsequently he called the priests into the city for seven days to attend a retreat, ending with a synod. As a step towards decentralization, he re-established the system of deaneries Bishop Power had begun. But he realized that the diocese was too big, and recommended that it be divided in three: Toronto with six counties and 40,000 Catholics; Hamilton with eight counties and 22,000 Catholics; and London with nine counties and 10,000 Catholics. This division took place in 1856.

Dealing with bigotry

In his request to Rome for this proposal, Charbonnel wrote, "Thank God our Irish know only how to believe in the Church, and Protestants make less noise than we could fear."4 But when he appealed for a division at the Second Council of Quebec in 1855, he revealed the problems his laity faced:

> Protestantism reigns supreme in the Diocese of Toronto, powerful, rich, and zealous; it has at its beck and call landed property, business, and labour, and numerous clergy, well endowed, teaching in schools of every branch and degree, churches and magnificent schools in abundance, elections and all the seats in Parliament, almost all public employment, houses of charity, the press and secret societies. (Meanwhile) the

> Bishop of Toronto is insulted in the streets of this
> city, and in several counties there have been dif-
> ferent attempts on the life of the missionaries.5

The Protestant majority in Toronto viewed the Famine Irish not only as an alien group but as worthy of contempt because of their Catholicism. As one man put it: "God has destroyed the Roman Catholics in the South and West of Ireland with famine and disease.... God gave them a final overthrow in the distant towns and other parts of North America."6

By the time Charbonnel arrived, this unsympathetic stereotype of the Irish made it difficult to obtain assistance for them. George Brown's *Globe* abused them constantly, as reported on 11 February 1858:

> Irish beggars are to be met everywhere, and
> they are as ignorant and vicious as they are poor.
> They are lazy, improvident, and unthankful; they
> fill our poor-houses and our prisons, and are as
> brutish in their superstition as Hindoos.

Charbonnel's response to Brown's biting remarks about his priests and to attacks against his flock on the streets was to try to build a separate society for them. The growth of Catholic churches, institutions, and solidarity naturally made the Protestants uneasy and even more hostile. But the bishop stood his ground. When the mayor of Toronto asked for a contribution to the Patriotic Fund in 1855, Charbonnel replied that the thousands of children in Toronto and the rest of his diocese who were intellectually starving and perishing because of want of religious education and the means necessary for it, and the thousands of immigrants whom the most unjust tyranny sent to Canada every year, had a prior claim on his charity.

The Religious Orders arrive

The Sisters of Loretto, excellent teachers but few in numbers, had already begun work in the two Catholic schools of Toronto. In 1851 the Sisters of St. Joseph arrived to take over

79

the orphanage which John Elmsley had established to protect the religion of the Famine Irish infants. They also began a program of outdoor relief and visitations to the homes of the poor, the sick, and the dying.

In 1855, Charbonnel opened the House of Providence, which was to become a crucible for social action under the administration of this dynamic group of nuns. It was a home for the orphaned, sick, aged, and destitute, run on a voluntary basis with the sisters begging for its maintenance both in the city and outside it. From this single institution begun by the bishop, there developed Providence Villa for the aged, three hospitals (St. Michael's, St. Joseph's, and Our Lady of Mercy), three orphanages, St. Nicholas Home for street boys, and Notre Dame for working girls—all under the care of the Sisters of St. Joseph.

At Charbonnel's invitation, the Christian Brothers arrived from France in 1851 to open St. Michael's College in the bishop's rectory, and to assist the Sisters of Loretto in teaching the primary grades. Later, they expanded their work to establish De La Salle High School and St. John's Training School. As a consequence, the training of skilled and educated young Irishmen proceeded at the hands of teachers whose methods were widely acclaimed.

In response to Charbonnel's plea for the establishment of a seminary in Canada West, the Basilian Fathers arrived in 1852. Charbonnel gave the Christian Brothers charge of the Catholic boys' schools in the city, and the Basilians the responsibility of administering the newly constructed St. Basil's Church and St. Michael's College, built on land donated by John Elmsley. Like the Christian Brothers, the Basilians were plagued with financial problems at the outset.

Clerics were subjected to the same persecution as the Irish population, but this only helped to draw the Catholic community in Toronto closer together. Raids against the St. Joseph's Orphanage especially provoked Catholic ire. The nuns who ran it were very dear to the Bishop's heart.

Working 14 to 16 hours a day, sharing beds with orphaned children and having barely enough to eat, they proved to the people that they too lived at subsistence level. Witnessing the mild response Charbonnel and his clergy gave to physical attack and verbal abuse, the laity adopted a similar attitude of Christian forbearance which alleviated some of the old tensions.

The St. Vincent de Paul Society

To supplement the work of the religious orders, Charbonnel required a lay organization to function in a voluntary manner, and he found it in the Society founded in France in 1833 by Alfred de Mun and Frederick Ozanam. Ozanam said,

Go to the poor, go to the worker. Go not with empty hands. And what is more, go live among the poor and the workers.

Members of the Society, established in Toronto in 1850, did not consider poverty a sin but a human condition that had to be overcome. The bishop often accompanied members on their visits, saying, "God loves the poor." He would lift his outer robe, the gift of a Toronto merchant, to reveal his tattered garments underneath, and this gesture uplifted the spirits of those who saw it.

Besides visiting the sick and the poor, the St. Vincent de Paul Society found living accommodation, paid rents, provided food, furnished tools for workers, and even established libraries to spread the faith and educate the poor. It influenced the formation of benevolent and insurance societies, and in 1890 it started what was to become the Catholic Children's Aid Society. Other societies were formed which were modelled along its lines, especially women's groups which supplied food and clothing to school children, assisted the nuns in various ways, and raised money for the religious orders.

Catholic schools and controversy

Even before his arrival in Toronto, Charbonnel had been told by Elmsley that "your arrival will be the commencement of a new era: ... religion and religious education will soon be planted upon the best possible footing."[7] One of his major goals was to secure Catholic schools for his flock. He soon concluded that only through a system of separate education could the Catholic children be kept as practising Catholics. He was determined to make this system independent of the common one, not wanting it based on an educational philosophy attuned to Protestantism.

When Charbonnel came to Toronto, there were only two Catholics schools, and he immediately asked for assistance to set up a school to accommodate the Catholic children who were allowed to run wild in the eastern portion of the city. He offered a reasonable compromise: the school would be staffed by the sisters and, therefore, would be operated at minimal cost, and it would help regenerate a class of children who might otherwise become criminals. But the city rejected his plan. This led him to become embroiled in a bitter conflict with Egerton Ryerson, the Methodist leader who was largely responsible for setting up the public school system in Ontario. Nonetheless, the bishop's own approach was not always popular with Catholics; they felt he was pressuring them to support a system of whose merits they were not convinced. But they began to support his stand more forcefully when they realized the implications of various pronouncements by Ryerson, particularly as they applied to Catholic teachers employed in the common schools.

A Lenten pastoral letter that Bishop Charbonnel issued in 1857 produced considerable controversy. It said that Catholic electors who did not use their electoral power on behalf of separate schools were guilty of mortal sin, as were confessors who gave absolution to parents who sent their children to mixed schools. The letter was especially directed against those in the hinterland who by their lack of support threatened the existence of Catholic schools. Most Irish Catholics in rural areas did compromise their religious principles and sent their children to mixed schools. Even the leading Catholic politician in the province, John Sandfield Macdonald from Glengarry, did not favour separate education and spoke out against it.[8]

In the urban centres, the Church was hard pressed to meet the demands of the growing lay population for separate schools. The Irish newspapers in Toronto supported the bishop's concept of Catholic schools throughout his tenure and well beyond. Still, the financial problems were enormous; Charbonnel had to use the residue of his personal estate from France to make up the deficit in the year 1854. But, one year after Charbonnel's departure, praise of Catholic teachers came from a strange and unexpected source. Egerton Ryerson admitted that the Sisters of St. Joseph and the Christian Brothers deserved recognition for the positive impact that they had in educating Catholic youth in Toronto, directing them towards virtue, morality and useful knowledge.[9]

The Bishop retires

In 1860, Bishop Charbonnel submitted his resignation as Bishop of Toronto. He may have been impelled to do so by the abuse directed towards him and his French Basilians because of their French accents and backgrounds. The abuse came from a small fraction of the urban Irish, yet it may have been a signal to the bishop of the need for change. He went back to France, and entered the Capuchin Order. His last gift to Toronto was an eminently qualified English-speaking bishop, John Joseph Lynch. Charbonnel was able to escort his successor to a place among the archbishops at the Vatican Council of 1870. The See which he himself had divided had now entered on a new dignity and importance: it was a metropolitan See, an archbishopric.

References:

1. Most of the data in this chapter were taken from M. W. Nicolson, *The Catholic Church and the Irish in Victorian Toronto*; see also M. W. Nicolson, *Bishop Charbonnel: the beggar bishop and the origins of Catholic social action* (Toronto: Canadian Catholic Historical Association, 1983), pp.51-66.

2. *The Canadian Freeman,* 14 May 1863.

3. *Dictionary of Canadian biography,* v.12 (Toronto: University of Toronto Press, 1990), pp.182-185.

4. Arcat, *Charbonnel papers,* Charbonnel to the Prefect of the Congregation of Propaganda, 25 May 1855.

5. *Ibid.,* Charbonnel to all the bishops during the Second Council of Quebec, 20 Oct. 1855.

6. Arcat, *Power papers,* A 'christian' to Rev. Mr. Carl [Carroll] , n.d.

7. Arcat, *Charbonnel papers,* S. G. Lynn and J. Elmsley to Charbonnel, July 1850.

8. For information on Bishop Charbonnel's involvement in the separate school issue see, for example: John S. Moir, *Church and state in Canada West* (Toronto: University of Toronto Press, 1959), pp.144-170; F. A. Walker, *Catholic education and politics in Ontario,* v.1 (Toronto: Dent, 1955), pp.76-218.

9. E. Ryerson, *Journal of education for Upper Canada,* v.14 (9), Sept. 1861.

CHAPTER EIGHT

WESTERN CANADA MISSIONS
1800-1880

In the pre-Confederation era, the vast western region of Canada was protected in its isolation from the outside influences of both Canada and the United States. It remained primarily in the hands of the nomadic Indians and the Métis, until the arrival of the railway in the late nineteenth century. That event allowed for the penetration of the Canadian West by various groups, with the consequence that diversity is a quality western provinces continue to share.

Perhaps the first Catholic presence in the North West was that of Father Charles Albanel, who travelled from Quebec to Hudson Bay in 1671. No missionaries followed him, but the Church expanded by having priests travel with the fur traders into the interior of the west. When the Hudson Bay basin was ceded to Britain in 1713, the explorer La Vérendrye, accompanied by a Jesuit, Charles Mesaiger, established a post at Portage la Prairie, where two additional Jesuits were assigned to work with the Indians and Métis.[1]

The intermarriage of white men with Indian women produced two distinct groups of mixed peoples that held influence in the West. One group, known as the English half-breeds, was mostly of Scottish and Indian mixture, English-speaking, and Protestant in religion. Looked upon as children of the Hudson's Bay Company, this group moved down from the north and settled in the Red River area. The other group was the Métis proper, known also as the Bois-Brûlé (Burnt Wood). The earliest origins of the group were among the voyageurs in the East, with an extended mixing through the trappers of the North West Company. They were French-speaking and Catholic.

Red River settlement

Both groups farmed on strips along river frontage, hunted buffalo, and utilized the Red River cart, constructed with high, wooden wheels to accommodate crossing marsh and plain. The greaseless axles caused a distinctive shriek of the wheels that could be heard for long distances. The noise of as many as twelve hundred carts signalled the movement of the Buffalo Hunt. Modes of transportation also included canoes, bateaux, and York boats, the latter a flat-bottomed boat designed by the English to carry heavier loads and fitted with sails for use on the larger lakes. As a staple dietary and trade item they produced pemmican, a dried meat mixed with berries. They communicated in a language called Bungay, comprised of English, French, and Indian. They intermarried and produced some strong leaders.

Paradoxically, the Protestant Lord Selkirk and his Scottish settlers on the Red River were instrumental in promoting Catholicism in the West. The wealthy Selkirk, who owned a large interest in the Hudson's Bay Company, wanted to improve the fortunes of landless Scottish crofters. He purchased a vast tract of land along the Assiniboine, Red, and Winnipeg Rivers and brought out Scottish emigrants to occupy the agricultural settlement he planned on the Red River. This area, however, was occupied illegally by the North West Fur Company and its employees—Catholic French Canadians and Métis, and Presbyterian Scottish half-breeds.

The presence of the Selkirk settlers, who began to arrive in 1812, was resented by the "Nor'westers" as a threat to the fur trade. Pressure on them to return east to Upper Canada included the offer of free transportation. The pressure succeeded through persistent harassment, culminating in 1816 in the Seven Oaks massacre of twenty-one settlers, which gave control of the colony to the Nor'westers. As a counter-measure, Selkirk hired Swiss and German mercenaries of the DeMeuron regiment, disbanded after the War of 1812-14, to restore the colony to his settlers.[2]

Lord Selkirk failed in his bid to obtain a Presbyterian minister for the Scottish settlers but, while in Montreal, advocated with Bishop J. Plessis to supply mission priests to the area to serve the needs of the French Canadians and the Swiss Catholic mercenaries. He followed up in 1817 by promising to give the Church 10,000 acres at the Red River. Plessis saw the opportunity of spreading Catholicism across the West and the potential for a bishopric subject to Quebec, but was hesitant to act in the face of Hudson's Bay Company and North West fur trade rivalries. At the direct request for a permanent mission however, Plessis sent Father Joseph Norbert Provencher, Jesuit Father N. Dumoulin, and a seminarian to the Red River in 1818. The priests worked hard to convince the voyageurs to settle their families and to adopt the strip-farming methods so common in Quebec. As a result, the Red River mission grew rapidly and was supplied with volunteer clergy from Provencher's old parish in Quebec. In acknowledgement of the civilizing influence the missionaries exercised, Provencher was made auxiliary to Bishop Plessis of Quebec.

Two major problems faced the new mission fields. One was a lack of resources and the second related to the 1818 British-United States agreement to establish the 49th parallel as the boundary. This agreement placed Father Dumoulin's Pembina mission and school in the United States, along with a vast territory and its Métis inhabitants. Provencher had spent time in the East, collecting resources for his missionary work, but was anxious to return west, particularly since the two rival fur companies had merged. In 1822, he was consecrated bishop and left that spring with the fur brigade.

St. Boniface

Provencher conducted religious services out of his

house in the area of the Red and Assiniboine Rivers. After 1822 he built a wooden church in the settlement called St. Boniface, in honour of the patron saint of the German-speaking Swiss mercenaries. This was to become a thriving mission, with schools and an Indian agricultural settlement, and, in 1848, as the seat of the Bishop of St. Boniface, its wooden church was replaced with a twin-towered stone cathedral. But in 1823 Plessis closed out Father Dumoulin's Pembina mission, which by then was beyond British control. The disheartened Dumoulin left the same year.[3]

Provencher succeeded in expanding the mission field among the natives, but keeping priests at the posts proved difficult. Loneliness, isolation, the nomadic lifestyle of the aboriginals, difficult circumstances and environmental extremes, and language barriers, were not conducive to success. Still by 1842 one priest had reached Fort Edmonton, where he remained for ten years. Another, however, Father Jean Darveau, was put to death in 1844 by the natives when he attempted to set up a permanent post at The Pas.[4]   And Father Georges Belcourt, who had established the first mission at St. Paul, Minnesota, in 1832, was dismissed in 1848 from Hudson's Bay Company territory for siding with the Métis against the company's tyrannical rule. He switched to the Pembina mission on American soil.[5]

Oblates of Mary Immaculate

Assistance came, in 1845, through the Oblates of Mary Immaculate, a French order of priests founded by Eugène de Mazenod in 1816, and approved by Rome in 1826. Provencher, who encountered the Order in Montreal, believed the future of the western church lay in their hands. Arriving with the first Oblate was a Canadian novice, Alexandre-Antonin Taché, who seemed too young to meet the demands of the tasks ahead. Yet, by 1846, the two priests had created a standing mission at Ile-à-la-

Crosse in Northern Saskatchewan, and, three years later, started another one on Lake Athabaska in Northern Alberta.

Even before he was thirty years old, Taché had been made Provencher's coadjutor. When the latter died in 1853, Taché took over as bishop of a diocese which covered two million square miles, with a staff of four diocesan priests and seven Oblates. Following Provencher's vision, Taché oversaw the opening of new missions at Lac la Biche, Lake Athabasca, and Nipigon, introducing ten Oblates and three Christian Brothers into the diocese. After personally evaluating the needs of the people in the northern missions, Taché planned to expand even further northward and sent a missionary to explore the Peace River district.

Taché could no longer cope on his own with the workload of the diocese from St. Boniface and, in 1859, was granted a coadjutor, Vital Grandin. The Oblates, in their vigour and eagerness, had taken charge of all diocesan work in the west and continued to open missions, so that by 1867 they had reached the Pacific and Arctic Oceans. Grandin had toured the northern missions from 1861 to 1864. More and closer supervision was required and, consequently, a vicar apostolic was appointed for Athabaska-Mackenzie in 1862, which opened the path for further diocesan structures towards the Rockies.[6]

Lac La Biche.

Grey nuns

While recognizing the evangelising contribution of the missionary priests, one must also credit the work of the Grey Nuns. Bishop Provencher requested their assistance, with the promise that a building would be erected in St. Boniface to serve as a house and school, with a garden behind. The Superior General of the order in Montreal agreed and arranged for four sisters to take up the post. Heavy baggage and supplies had to be sent to England, then back by sea to a trading post on Hudson Bay, and then south by boatmen to the Red River.

The four nuns set out by canoe with eight voyageurs on April 24, 1844, from Lachine, Montreal, on an arduous journey, along the Ottawa River to Lake Nipissing, across Lake Huron to Sault Ste. Marie, across Lake Superior to Fort William, then west via narrow rivers and steep portages to Lake of the Woods, on to the Winnipeg River and south to the Red River, arriving at St. Boniface at 1:00 a.m. on June 21, 1844. Within three weeks, the sisters had opened a school in their house for fifty-four Métis girls, and one for younger boys in the basement of the bishop's house; later they opened an industrial school where older girls and women were taught household skills like spinning, weaving, knitting, and sewing. One of the nuns drove from home to home, teaching those unable to attend school. By 1848 the sisters had a new, much bigger, and more comfortable convent. Programs in the new premises soon burgeoned. By 1862, Father Joseph Ritchot was able to report that the sisters were providing care for about fifty orphans, "boys and girls who come from every part of the diocese ... Métis of every possible origin: Irish, Cree, Saulteaux, Montagnais, and even Sioux." With pride, he also observed: "As to the pupils of the boarding school, I dare say that the examination results could honour our fine convents in Lower Canada. The program of studies is exactly the same: French, English, history, mathematics, drawing and music."[7]

Nursing was another important aspect of the Grey Nuns' work. Having learned as much practical medicine as they could before leaving Montreal, they could not ignore the sick, whose needs became evident as the sisters travelled door-to-door.

Their abilities were put to the test in 1846 when the Red River settlement was struck with one disease after another. They closed the schools for a period to focus on the sick, visiting homes and arranging for the most ill to be brought to St. Boniface. In one three-week period, there were ninety-six deaths as a result of "bloody flux", and comforting the bereaved became an important part of their mission.

The following year, one of the rooms in the convent was opened as a hospital ward. But for the most part, nursing care was done in the homes of the sick; in their first decade, the sisters made over 6,000 visits in the settlement. Occasionally, medicines arrived from Montreal, but often the sisters made poultices, ointments, and remedies of every description from the resources at hand: mint, pumpkin, rhubarb, black currants, milkweed, cherry bark, spruce sap, goldenrod, blood root, wild strawberry, and corn tassels.

By 1854 there were eleven sisters in the convent at St. Boniface and two at St. François-Xavier at White Horse Plain, a settlement established by the Métis leader, Cuthbert Grant. In their fawn-coloured habits, with moccasins on their feet, the nuns, who rebounded from every adversity, won the hearts of the Métis and Indians they served. Their numbers gradually increased, especially with novices from among the girls they educated, who bore names like Connolly, Goulet, McDougall, St. Laurent, Riel—reflecting their varied Métis backgrounds. Like the Oblates, the Grey Nuns advanced their missionary endeavours westward and northward through hard work and a willingness to accept multiple cultures.

The Métis

While the Métis accepted the advantages the missionaries provided, by 1850 they were becoming alarmed at the social and environmental changes affecting their lifestyle. The buffalo were not as plentiful, and competition for this major food source intensified between the Métis and the Indian tribes. Moreover, the rules governing the buffalo hunt were the basis of the Métis social structure, and collapse of the hunt jeopardized the fabric of their community. Their carts and canoes were being replaced by modernized shipping and transportation methods, which invited increased settlement and threatened their land ownership. Their response to these issues had far-reaching consequences in the political sphere, sometimes placing the Church in a difficult position.

Among the Métis were strong leaders including Cuthbert Grant, Warden of the Plains; Gabriel Dumont; Pierre Falcon; John Bruce; Ambrose Lepine; Louis Riel, senior; and, most memorable, his son Louis Riel. As a boy, the young Louis Riel was educated at the College of Montreal, but did not enter the priesthood as Taché had expected. He returned to the Red River at the time the North West was being transferred from the Hudson's Bay Company to Canada. These arrangements were concluded without consulting the majority Métis, who were concerned that the survey methods used in Ontario would reduce their holdings. The Métis, under the leadership of Riel, seized Upper Fort Garry (Winnipeg) and formed a provisional government. They formulated a Bill of Rights, which protected their language, religion, and farms, upon which Ottawa negotiated the Manitoba Act in 1870, creating the province.

Thomas Scott, an Orangeman from Ontario, was jailed along with a group of English-speaking trouble-makers who refused to recognize the authority of the provisional government. Scott continued to be abusive to the guards and was shot by the Métis, under their code of acceptable behaviour. Ottawa held Riel accountable for Scott's death and dispatched an army under Colonel Garnett Wolseley to assume control of the new province. Riel prudently went south to the United States, where he taught school until he was called north, in 1885, to assume the leadership of the Métis and Indians, whose conditions had worsened.

Saskatchewan

If Manitoba's growth was slow, it seems that Saskatchewan's was even slower. However, a mission was established among the Chipeywan and Cree in Ile-à-la-Crosse, in 1846, by Taché and Rev. Louis LaFleche, a diocesan priest. Ile-à-la-Crosse was a vital trading centre and a coveted site among the Anglicans, Wesleyans and Catholics for missionary activity, all of whom sought to be first to evangelize the Dene (the Chipeywans). The Hudson's Bay Company was opposed to mission settlements in case they might upset the trading habits of the Indians. But the Chief Factor of the Post at Ile-à-la-Crosse knew that the Cree and the Chipeywan hunters were anxious to learn about Christianity and, he believed, the added feature of a misisonary would keep them 'trading at' his post, rather than drifting toward the Plains.[8] And Oblates served the community all during those years, with faith in God, devotion to Mary, and dedication to prayer and family life paramount. Nine Oblates are buried in its graveyard, as are eight Grey Nuns, among them Louis Riel's sister.

The Grey Nuns came to the village in 1860. After a rough journey from St. Boniface that took 63 days, the Grey Nuns came to Ile-à-la-Crosse in 1860 with Bishop Vital Grandin. Immediately, the nuns became engrossed in teaching, nursing, and caring for orphans. Cree, Dene, French, and English were the languages spoken at the mission. From this site, other missions evolved, each threatened with famine, fire, disease, and flood. It was not until the later decades of the 19th century that a substantial population growth began to occur in Saskatchewan.

Among the traders of the North West Company attracted to the fur-rich west was John Rowand, the son of a Scottish surgeon in Montreal and a French-Canadian mother. From early in the nineteenth century, Rowand worked between Lake Winnipeg and the Rocky Mountains. He became head of the Hudson's Bay Company's Saskatchewan District and ruled the plains from his headquarters at Fort Edmonton. A Catholic, educated at the Sulpician College in Montreal, Rowand had an overwhelming experience in working with Indians and Métis, and his friendship was to be a boon to Father Albert Lacombe, whose name is bound firmly to the history of Alberta.

Fr. Albert Lacombe, missionary to the North West

Father Lacombe, a Quebec farm boy, carried the blood of the voyageurs and of a Métis grandmother. Educated in Montreal and ordained to the priesthood in 1849, the young Lacombe was stirred by the exploits of Father Georges Belcourt from the Pembina mission, who came seeking financial help for the Indians and Métis. Lacombe was given permission to return with Belcourt to Pembina, where he spent two summers before being recalled to Montreal. This gave him the opportunity of learning to speak Salteux and experiencing, first-hand, the strict rules governing the Métis buffalo hunt.

Inspired by the Oblates, their self-denial and accommodation, Lacombe believed he needed the discipline and support of such an Order to pursue his dream. But he had little time to ponder the move, for Taché was in Montreal in 1852, begging for priests. He accepted Lacombe as a volunteer to return with him—promising that the young man could make his novitiate as an Oblate at St. Boniface. Within 24 hours of his arrival at St. Boniface, however,

Lacombe was told to take over the unattended mission post at Fort Edmonton. It was on this journey that John Rowand became mentor to the young Lacombe, teaching him about the pemmican posts, the trade routes, the habits and make-up of the various native tribes, and the difficult conditions under which they lived. Lacombe became friend to the Crees and Blackfoot, helping to establish reserves and schools, and to quell tribal tensions and calm Métis tempers. With Father Constantine Scollen, an Irishman who set up the first English school at Fort Edmonton in 1862, Lacombe composed a dictionary and prayer book for the Blackfoot, and a dictionary and grammar for the Cree.

Known as the "Black Robe Voyageur", Lacombe had a parish covering 250,000 square miles. Small-pox devastated the mixed population of Alberta in 1870, and the relentless care which Lacombe and his brother Oblates and the ailing Bishop Grandin provided to the sick and dying left a lasting impression. When Father Lacombe died in 1916 in his beloved Alberta, the whole of the West mourned.

British Columbia: initial evangelization

The French and Métis promoted Catholic evangelization along the British Columbia coast. As employees of the Northwest/Hudson's Bay Company, they settled along two tributaries of the Columbia River at Fort Vancouver, in the current Oregon. They asked Bishop Provencher for priests in 1834 and again in 1835, but the Hudson's Bay Company denied the request, most likely because of the presence in the area of five American Methodist ministers. In 1838, however, Provencher was allowed to send, from Red River, Fathers E. Blanchet and Modeste Demers, provided their mission was located north of the territory claimed by the expanding United States. No Catholic priests had been in that area since the Spanish friars had left more than 50 years before.

Father Demers was responsible for the northern territory of the mission. In 1841, travelling to Fort Langley on the Fraser River, Demers and Blanchet discovered a nearby Jesuit mission under the jurisdiction of the Bishop of St. Louis. They decided upon a division of labour, and Demers began an extended journey of a year up the Columbia River to Stuart Lake. His purpose was to penetrate the mainland in advance of the Protestant clergy. In effect, Fr. Demers baptized about 280 Indians. Other than the contributions of the Jesuits, who were recalled to the southern regions in 1848, there was no further sustained effort at Catholic evangelization in the interior of British Columbia until the arrival of the Oblates in 1859. Sporadic episodes included that of Father Jean-Baptiste Bolduc who accompanied the future governor, James Douglas, on his second voyage to Vancouver Island in 1843. In that year Bolduc baptized a large number of Songhees; unfortunately there was no significant follow-up.

For 57 years of its existence, Victoria was a suffragan See under the influence of Oregon. When he was consecrated Bishop of Vancouver Island in 1847, Demers' jurisdiction was a wilderness that encompassed all of British Columbia and north to the Arctic Ocean. He spent the first four years of his tenure abroad in an ineffective attempt to secure clergy before setting up residence in Victoria in 1852. In the political sphere, Victoria was the capital of Vancouver Island under the governorship of James Douglas. When the 1858 gold rush to the Fraser River attracted hordes of American prospectors and camp-followers, the British Government created a colony, British Columbia, on the mainland, making James Douglas governor. Troops and lawmakers were sent in to establish order.

Two other significant events occurred in 1858. The Sisters of St. Anne from Quebec arrived in Victoria to establish schools, orphanages, and hospitals. And the Oblates moved their Pacific headquarters to Esquimalt, establishing St. Joseph's Mission. From this post, the superior, Louis-Joseph D'Herbomez, oversaw the development of a succession of

Oblate missionary posts on the British Columbia mainland, hoping to forestall the advance of Anglican measures.

In 1864 D'Herbomez was made bishop of New Westminster, taking in the entire mainland of British Columbia, separated from the Diocese of Vancouver Island, and leaving the area under total Oblate control. At that time, Americans formed the majority population in Victoria and it was not until 1903 that the connection between the Province of Oregon and the Vancouver diocese was broken.

The initial phases of Catholic evangelization in the West were carried out by French personnel, either from France or Quebec, with very little evidence of English speakers until the late nineteenth century. In an era of great bigotry, the majority English in central Canada feared the dominance and potential power-base of the West's Catholic francophones. It is questionable whether the religious and cultural identities could be separated. Most appropriate, therefore, are Bishop Grandin's reflections: "The Indians call Catholicism the French religion and Protestantism the English religion. It is the truth for many of the public figures with whom I have had dealings; religion is for them more a matter of nationality than of conviction . . .To be a true English subject, one must be Protestant. . . ."[9]

References:

1. Arthur S. Morton, *A history of The Canadian West to 1870/71* (Toronto: University of Toronto Press, 1973), pp.70-77; 176.
2. W. L. Morton, *Manitoba: a history* (Toronto: University of Toronto Press, 1967), pp.55-56.
3. John S. Moir, *The Church in the British era* (Toronto: McGraw-Hill Ryerson, 1972), pp.196-200.
4. A. G. Morice, O.M.I., *History of the Catholic Church in Western Canada*, v.1 (Toronto: Musson, 1910), pp.176-180.
5. Alvin C. Gluek, Jr., *Minnesota and the manifest destiny of the Canadian Northwest* (Toronto: University of Toronto Press, 1965), pp.57-59; 72-74; 104-105.
6. For a history of the Oblates in the West, see Raymond J. A. Huel, *Proclaiming the Gospel to the Indians and the Métis* (Edmonton:

University of Alberta Press, 1996).

7. Dennis King, *The Grey Nuns and the Red River settlement* (Book Society of Canada, 1980), pp.36; 38.

8. Martha McCarthy, *From the great river to the ends of the earth. Oblate Missions to the Dene, 1847-1921* (Edmonton: University of Alberta Press, 1995), pp.32-33.

9. Robert Choquette, *The Oblate assault on Canada's Northwest* (Ottawa: University of Ottawa Press, 1995), p.205.

CHAPTER NINE

WESTERN CANADA

The Gospel takes root

Initially, evangelization of the West was contested by French-speaking Catholics and English-speaking Anglicans. The latter, as representatives of the established church, received strong support from the Hudson's Bay Company. But Catholic priests and nuns were more successful with the Indians and Métis because of an unencumbered lifestyle that permitted mobility. Their Anglican counterparts, with their families, were more reliant on possessions, which tended to fetter them in settled areas like the Red River colony.

Bishop Vital Grandin.

What shifted the French-Catholic, English-Protestant balance into the latter's favour was a failure to attract francophones from Quebec and New England to accept the offer of available land. The challenge was taken up by Protestant homesteaders, particularly from Ontario and the United States, already exposed to settlers' hardships. They were accompanied by young Presbyterian and Methodist ministers, devout farm boys who were not afraid to open up new territory. As for the English-speaking Catholic population, it, by contrast, was small, yet contained some fairly influential members able to provide strength to the Catholic cause of the French clergy.

Winnipeg, the door to the Prairies, was based on the Red River settlements, St. Boniface and Upper Fort Garry, with a mixture of Indian, Métis, French, English, Scots, and

Swiss-German. In 1867, the new Dominion of Canada was fearful of the intentions of the United States. With the end of the American Civil War in 1865, there was a possibility that American soldiers would march north to take Canada. Therefore, when Riel and his Métis followers rebelled, Canada hastened to create the new province of Manitoba, making Winnipeg its capital, and dispatching Colonel G. Wolseley to establish a military presence.

The arduous route to the West by Wolseley and his soldiers demonstrated the need for improved transportation. The Canadian government had promised a coach road, to be replaced later by a railway, linking Manitoba with British Columbia. Based upon this promise, the government of British Columbia asked to become a province of Canada in 1871, in an attempt to cut off American expansion. Winnipeg, then, gained prominence in western development.

Louis Riel

Many of the positive features in the social and political organization of the Red River derived from the work of the Catholic Church. They were transmitted to the new province of Manitoba. Instrumental in the achievement was Louis Riel, whose safety was in jeopardy after the arrival of the military. Riel subsequently took refuge in the United States, where he married, taught school, and became an American citizen. But, when in the 1880s the condition of the natives of the western plains deteriorated to the point that they were starving, Riel came north at the request of the Métis to forge an alliance among the tribes and his people. Hoping to replicate his Manitoba success, Riel sent a Bill of Rights to Ottawa. It was ignored.

Together with Gabriel Dumont, his military commander, Riel led a second rebellion against the Canadian government in 1885. This rebellion caused the railway project, which had been stalled because of financial difficulties, to be pushed forward to Winnipeg. British General F.

Middleton and his troops travelled by Red River cart from there to central Saskatchewan and the battle of Batoche. The rebellion was crushed, the Indians and the Métis demoralized. While Gabriel Dumont rode south to the United States, Riel remained, giving himself up for trial to plead the cause of his people.

Riel's trial had repercussions that divided the country along linguistic and religious lines which still reverberate today. Riel, who showed some signs of mental instability and who had relinquished the practice of his Catholic religion for a time, was sent to Regina, where he was sentenced to death for treason. The indictment against him read like a charge of witchcraft. The treason charge was questionable because Riel was an American citizen at the time. Moreover, the state of his sanity was at issue. Despite pleas to have the death sentence overturned, Prime Minister Sir John A. Macdonald, in 1885, declared: "He shall hang though every dog in Quebec bark in his favour." Riel's death sentence created a backlash against the Conservative Party in Quebec which lasted for decades.

Riel made peace with his God. Accompanied by Father Alexis André, the Oblate who had opposed Riel's efforts for the Métis in the past, but who became his confessor and companion in the death-watch, Riel mounted the scaffold. Ironically, the hangman had been a prisoner in Fort Garry during the first rebellion in 1870, and swore then to take revenge on Riel for his humiliation and for the death of his friend Thomas Scott. Riel was hanged in Regina in November 1885. After three weeks' delay, the government released his body to be shipped back to St. Boniface for a funeral Mass and burial.[1]

Winnipeg

The completion of the railway as a consequence of Riel's actions had a tremendous impact on Winnipeg. The town grew rapidly and land prices skyrocketed. Boarding houses were common as living space was limited, and overcrowding was an issue that disturbed the city fathers. Hotels, poolhalls, and houses of prostitution sprung up to attract the business of the new arrivals. The railways which made Winnipeg the "gateway to the West" also helped to make it become known as the "vice capital of Canada."

Included in the incoming groups of immigrants were the Irish, increasing the English-speaking component of the Catholic population. While the English-French duality of Manitoba was being broken by the influx of people from various backgrounds and nationalities—German, Swedish, Norwegian, Icelandic, Danish, Latvian—the composition of the Catholic laity diversified even further with the addition of Slavic peoples, especially Ukrainians, many of them Catholics of the Eastern rite.

Disturbing social problems were associated with the arrival of so many new Canadians, some of whom were dumped and forgotten in Winnipeg. Juvenile delinquency among the foreign born was a major concern. In response, ethno-religious hatred was promoted by many groups and individuals, a mind-set that had produced societies like the Protestant Protective Association in the 1890s, much as the Orange Order had evolved earlier in Ontario. Even J. S. Woodsworth, the former Methodist minister who was to gain renown as a Canadian social reformer and politician, believed, for example, that all Poles were Catholics of a fanatical type, and that Mormons were enemies of Anglo-Saxon civilization.

Immigration began in the early 1890s, leaving hundreds of families in a destitute condition when the real estate boom collapsed in 1913. Winnipeg city authorities established a welfare system, with all churches cooperating in the distribution of food. Regardless of these altruistic efforts, demands for deportation of aliens were heard from church and lodge.

The war years (1914-1918) heralded further discrimination against central Europeans, especially Germans and

Ukrainians from Austrian regions. No effort was made to determine ethnic origins; a general label of 'foreigner' or 'Galician' was applied and all were treated with disdain.[2]

Three archdioceses

Language and rite differences among Winnipeg's Catholics culminated in the city's unique situation of accommodating three independent archdiocesan structures. The Archdiocese of St. Boniface, the oldest in western Canada, retained a pre-eminent position until 1915 and has continued to the present as a francophone centre for the whole prairie region, sending its priests and bishops throughout Saskatchewan, Alberta, and British Columbia.

Meanwhile, the Irish were becoming restless. By 1906, the Irish were the predominent parishioners at St. Mary's Church, which had been established in 1876. They petitioned their French archbishop, A. Langevin of St. Boniface, to improve services to English-speakers by requesting the creation of additional English parishes, by securing English-speaking priests and even a bishop, and by establishing an English Catholic college. But nothing happened until 1915 when Langevin died. Rome, having recognized the growth of the English settlers, announced the creation of the new Archdiocese of Winnipeg, with A. A. Sinnot as first archbishop.

Similarly, the Ukrainian Catholics began to build churches before there were clergy to serve them. They appealed to Archbishop Langevin to obtain priests for them, primarily to end the seepage of Ukrainian Catholics into the ranks of the Ukrainian Orthodox Church, both following the Byzantine rite. The Vatican appointed Bishop Nykyta Budka to the newly formed Archeparchy of Winnipeg in 1912. And while Archbishop Langevin tried to settle the issues of rival Catholic groups, he was also embroiled in deeper, ethno-religious problems related to education.[3]

The Manitoba school question

One of the first statutes passed by the Manitoba Legislature in 1871 was an education act. It contained a pre-confederation arrangement whereby Catholic and Protestant denominational schools would each be supported by their own taxpayers. In addition, the two school systems were to share proportionately in provincial grants. This was suitable in 1871, when Manitoba's population was 11,000, about equally divided between French Catholics and English Protestants. Within 20 years, however, the population grew to 152,000, with Catholics numbering 22,800, or about 15% of the population.

It was not until 1890 that change occurred with the passing of the Public School Act and Department of Education Act. All prior acts were repealed and all denominational school property was appropriated. The new system, primarily of Protestant orientation, would receive all educational funds. The Catholic minority considered this a breach of rights under Section 22 of the Manitoba Act which had created the province. They sought redress in the courts. The judgement acknowledged that Catholics were taxed to support schools not in accordance with the rules and principles of their church. A government appeal was forwarded to the Privy Council in Britain which ruled that the legislature had the authority to enact the Public School Act, despite the consequences.

The Manitoba Catholics then petitioned the federal government for a remedial order, requiring the province to restore what they perceived as their constitutional rights. Again the Privy Council ruled that there would be no aid for denominational schools and, in fact, assessment for school purposes would not be destined for Catholic institutions. In 1895, the federal government passed a remedial order directing Manitoba to restore to Catholics the rights enjoyed prior to 1890, but the provincial government refused to comply. Subsequently, a bill was introduced to restore the rights, but was lost when Parliament in Ottawa dissolved for a general election.

Prime Minister Wilfrid Laurier met with Premier T. Greenway of Manitoba in 1896. An agreement was reached allowing limited religious instruction, the employment of Catholic teachers, and the use of a language other than English, under certain conditions. However, no share of public funds would be allocated to Catholic schools. These agreements were unsatisfactory to the Catholic minority and to Archbishop Langevin and a number of the Catholic hierarchy across Canada. Laurier asked Rome to stop the bishops' attacks against his government. The apostolic delegate, Msgr. Merry del Val, mediated, and the situation was resolved when the hierarchy agreed to comply with an encyclical letter from the Pope, asking for moderation.[4]

The Manitoba Catholics wanted their own schools, convinced a better education was offered than in many of the public ones, especially where there were disadvantaged students. The emphasis on a common academic core of work, the development of a strong social bond and a sense of community, coupled with a moral mission that involved personal responsibility, prepared students to meet the challenges of a hostile majority. But Winnipeg's Anglo-Saxon Protestant community wanted the absorption of both Catholic and Orthodox foreign elements and considered education the means for the accomplishment of this.

One problem was that Anglo-Saxon teachers refused employment in foreign districts. Both French and Ukrainian Catholics requested bilingual instruction—one to retain language, the other to retain the Byzantine rite identity under the umbrella of the larger Latin-rite Catholic adherence. The Protestant majority believed the French clergy agitated for special instruction and vented their anger against them when teachers were sought by both groups. The provincial government established Polish and

Ukrainian but not French training schools, and the Ukrainians created their own teacher organizations.[5]

British Columbia

The Catholic population in British Columbia has always been the lowest in Canada. Considering the importance of Catholic schools in safeguarding a religious heritage, British Columbia has had a difficult struggle. Prior to Confederation, the Oblates, the Sisters of St. Anne, and the Irish Christian Brothers had established Catholic schools, but these were exempt from funding under the clauses of the first Public School Act. Included, however, in the provision of federal funds were mission schools where Indian children were taught and boarded.

In 1881, British Columbia's three bishops petitioned the legislative assembly, pointing out the unfairness of Catholics having to pay public school taxes in addition to maintaining their own schools. Moreover, in the bishops' opinion, the abolition of religious instruction by school law was an injustice to those who wanted it. It took more than a hundred years for a partial redress. In 1989 funding for Catholic schools was increased to 50%, if all the schools (73 in the province) met basic standards, taught the approved curriculum, and hired certified teachers.

References:

1. Much has been written of Louis Riel. In particular, see George F. G. Stanley, *Louis Riel* (Toronto: Ryerson Press, 1962); Hartwell Bowsfield, ed., Louis Riel: *Rebel of the western frontier or victim of politics and prejudice?* (Toronto: Copp Clark, 1969).

2. Alan FJ. Artibise, *Winnipeg*: a social history of urban growth ,1874-1914 (Montreal: McGill-Queen's University Press, 1975).

3. John Webster Grant, *The Church in the Canadian era* (Welch Pub., 1988), pp.97-98.

4. Lovell Clark, *The Manitoba school question: majority rule or minority rights?* (Toronto: Copp Clark, 1968).

CHAPTER TEN

THE IRISH WORKER IN VICTORIAN TORONTO

By 1850 Toronto was burdened with a number of social and economic problems related to the sudden influx of 1847-1848 "Famine Irish" immigrants. The Protestant population viewed the minority group of predominantly Catholic working-class people as an alien element. The Irish worker was at a disadvantage within the growing city, for the emerging labour organizations were secret oath-bound societies antagonistic to Catholicism.

Though the Church had little political or economic power, it aided the adjustment of its laity who had to cope in a strongly anti-Catholic and anti-Irish environment. Fully cognizant of the injustice working men encountered, the Church came to terms with labour organizations in the 1880's and eased the entrance of its workers into them. (See the following chapter.)

The situation

Victorian Toronto's working class represented two distinctive cultural backgrounds: the majority Protestants whose quickly secularizing religion had become a culture, and an Irish peasant culture which had become a religion tied to the institutional Church.

Canadian labour history tends to exclude religion as a contributing factor to the study of working-class history. The important role Gregory Kealey, for example, assigns to the Orange Order in the development of labour organizations between 1867 and 1892 may well be accurate. However, it was instrumental in the development of a Protestant working-class culture.[1] The Jubilee riots in Toronto in 1875, when Orange mobs attacked Irish Catholics, typified religious bigotry and working-class disunity. Kealey contends that within a decade of the Riots the old sectarian quarrels between Orange and Green were left behind. With the Orange Order in control of a large section of the working class, however, unity was illusionary and fleeting at best. Irish Catholic workers survived in the realm of a counter-culture.

The relationship of the Church with the Irish worker in Toronto was an evolutionary one. Prior to the Famine migration in 1847-48, the Irish Catholic population had been a small, scattered group with minor concentrations in lower Cabbage Town, on the waterfront and Don flats. With the exception of a small middle sector of entrepreneurs, the group was composed chiefly of day labourers, carters, and a transient labour force employed in public works in the city and the province. Since these Irish workers had been detached from their Church in Ireland during penal times, superstition played a large role in their lives and they could hardly be described as 'Catholic' in the traditional sense. Without a church or a priest to lead them until the late 1820s, the indifferent Irish in Toronto were fast assimilating into the larger population.

Bishop Michael Power

When Toronto was established as a diocesan See in 1842, Bishop Michael Power concentrated on the external signs of episcopal presence by building a cathedral and bishop's palace. Through the construction of the cathedral, the Church became an urban actor and gave the Irish labourer a chance to diversify his skills.

St. Michael's Cathedral was constructed under the direction of the English-born architect William Thomas. The Irish laity volunteered what few pennies they could afford, as well as labour, carts, horses, lumber, bricks, and stone, and in the process learned new trades under Thomas' guidance. From that experience there evolved a group of building contractors who became proficient in the construction trades and later found employment in the emerging period of church and institutional building fostered by Bishop Armand de Charbonnel and his successors. Those contractors expanded their activities as industrial and residential building increased with the growth of the city. Furthermore, the construction of the cathedral gave rise to a group of Irish Catholic entrepreneurs who set up shop to supply the needs of the Church and the labourers. That helped to expand and diversify the middle sector of their population, and from it evolved a group of undertakers and professional men to service the close-knit Irish community.

The arrival of the Famine Irish immigrants changed the nature of the Irish Catholic population and broke the Protestant consensus in the city. Irish Catholics increased from 2,000 to 7,940 by 1851, forming 25.8 percent of Toronto's population. By 1900 the Catholics, still predominantly Irish, numbered 28,994 and at 13.9 percent formed a small working-class minority in a city of just over 200,000 inhabitants.

Both the city and the Church were ill-prepared to cope with the social problems of the Famine immigrants. While the city hid in fear of the contagion they brought, Bishop Power died as a result of it as he and his few priests ministered to their needs in the fever sheds on the wharves. A three-year leaderless interregnum followed Power's death, during which time the structural organization of the Church fell into abeyance, with Gallican Irish priests throughout the diocese defying the authority of the temporary administrators. Material aid was almost non-existent and the immigrants were left at the mercy of the city's charities.

Bishop Charbonnel

Armand de Charbonnel, the second Bishop of the Diocese of Toronto, made change a sine qua non. Living as a beggar, his lifestyle no better than that of the poorest Irish labourer in his flock, he made the Irish his people and set the standard for self-sacrifice by giving his family fortune to the Church and the Irish poor.

Charbonnel vigorously initiated a two-fold program: the reorganization of the Church government and the creation of institutions to aid the deprived Irish working class. He divided the vast diocese into three interlocking units, which reduced the span of control and allowed him to concentrate more fully on the problems of Toronto and its

St. Basil's Church at St. Michael's College.

immediate hinterland. Evaluating the deplorable conditions of his impoverished laity, ill, starving, and freezing, Charbonnel utilized the Church's network to obtain funds, religious orders of priests, nuns and brothers, and the model for a lay organization, the St. Vincent de Paul Society, to serve them.

St. Vincent de Paul Society

The first St. Vincent de Paul Council established in the city in 1850 was dominated by the old, non-Irish Catholic elite. Its purpose as a voluntary organization was to dispense charity and to assist in the social and religious reorganization of the deprived laity. Beginning with a program of simple outdoor relief in which the members visited the

110

poor and supplied food, clothing, fuel, medicine, and shelter, the Society soon gained the confidence of those it served. Because the members met the poor as equals, not as social observers, it was a society without class structure. But it eventually became an Irish working-class association. With Irish aiding Irish in the name of their Church, the Society became a vital element in the spread of Irish urban culture.

The members of the St. Vincent de Paul Society gained entrance to the hospitals for the sick, paid rent and taxes for injured and sick workmen, provided tools for workers, and found lodgings for transient labourers. They visited the jails and assisted in the rehabilitation of prisoners, set up libraries and distributed books and papers, ran night schools for untrained adults, and, to assure the education of the future generation, acted as unpaid truant officers in the emerging separate school system. In an attempt to direct the Irish towards means of self-help, the Society promoted housing co-operatives and established a fuel co-operative, an employment agency, and, with the Bishop, a Savings Bank to encourage planning for old age, children's education, and times of illness and unemployment. And to protect the religious rights of Irish Catholics, the Society was instrumental in the formation of the St. Vincent de Paul Children's Aid Society.

Women's Irish societies

Parish-oriented women's organizations developed in a similar manner, complementing the work of the St. Vincent de Paul Society. The first was instituted during the period of interregnum to set up an orphanage, employing immigrant Irish girls to care for infants who would otherwise be placed in Protestant homes by the charitable organizations of the city. From bazaars and picnics, the various women's groups obtained food and clothing which they then supplied to school children, as well as glasses, books, and sundry items to hospital patients and female prisoners. They became involved in visiting the jails and courts, and aided in the social adjustment of released female prisoners.

However, it was the religious orders which were central to the expansion of a program for Irish Catholic social action. The Sisters of St. Joseph arrived from France in 1851 to assume control of the existing orphanage. They, like the St. Vincent de Paul Society, set up a system of outdoor relief, visited the homes of the sick, and began to teach in the schools. By 1900 they had developed the House of Providence, three orphanages, St. Michael's Hospital, St. Nicholas Institute for newsboys and apprentices, and Notre Dame des Anges as a boarding home for girls. In addition, they administered and taught in a number of schools. And, with the St. Vincent de Paul Society, they were instrumental in the formation of the Catholic Children's Aid Society.

Other orders, like the Sisters of Charity and the Good Shepherds community provided care for destitute women and prostitutes and set up industrial schools to train young girls.

The sons of the Irish working class were educated by the Basilian Fathers and the Christian Brothers. The Christian Brothers established St. John's Industrial School, where young boys in trouble with the law were taught skills that equipped them to enter the labour force. Because of the close interaction between the religious orders and the Irish working class, a bond grew between the people and the Church. As the orders drew postulants from those they served, they too eventually became Irish in composition.[2]

Anti-Catholic sentiment

The Famine Irish had created a surplus of labour in the city, and it was generally believed that they would hire themselves at lower wages. Protestant workers felt threatened, and vented their frustrations against the Church. She had been tolerated when she was weak and subservient; when new church buildings, rectories, schools, and social institutions showed clearly her power and cohesion with Irish Catholics, her activity was viewed as a papal conspiracy. But it was the demand for separate schools—and the economic consequence of them—that became the major issue.

With the aid of George Brown's newspaper *The Globe*, Egerton Ryerson, and the Orange Lodge, a Protestant Crusade began and the Irish community was under harsh pressure. Commenting on its results, *The Mirror* of April 3, 1857, wrote:

> *Catholic servants, Catholic labourers, Catholic merchants have all felt the effect in their business relations. They have seen with pain, not unnoticed with indignation, that every fresh move on the Separate School question, subjugated them—more or less—to reprisal of Protestant spleen and purgatorial malignity.*

In 1848, the influential Ryerson, observing the plight of the Famine Irish, expressed the belief that the "physical disease and death which have accompanied this influx among us may be the precursor of the worst pestilence of social insubordination and disorder." He was convinced that immigrants, particularly those from Ireland, were as "notoriously destitute of intelligence and industry as they are of means of subsistence"[3], thereby contributing to crime. Throughout his career, Ryerson's Journal of education persisted in an anti-Irish, anti-Catholic approach in the separate school conflict. The writings of Brown and Ryerson helped unite the Orange Lodge, the Protestant pulpit, the press, the public schools, and the work place against the Irish Catholic working class.

Facing such strong ethno-religious opposition, these workers had great difficulty in finding employment in the city. With the consensus that 'No Irish Need Apply', the Irish Catholic press reported on the differential treatment. As an example, Irish Catholics were refused work, as well as lodgings in boarding houses. And an advertisement for the Burnside Lying-In Hospital stipulated that applicants for matron "must be Protestant". In a satirical vein, the Irish press replied that it would be advantageous if "she [the matron] was something of a vocalist, and had by heart select Orange tunes such as 'Protestant Boys' or 'Croppies Lie Down'."[4]

When, in 1865, a motion was put forward to allow the Sisters of the House of Providence the use of the Crystal Palace for a charitable function, Mayor F. Medcalfe was reported to have said that "whenever Roman Catholics or their religion were encouraged, the community suffered.... Should we allow the statement that we encouraged Catholics to go forth to the world?"[5]

The Orange Lodge

The Orange Order had its roots as an English secret society, formed about 1686, to promote the revolution that replaced the Catholic, King James II, with his Protestant daughter Mary and her husband William of Orange. In 1690, William secured the submission of Ireland at the Battle of the Boyne. Subsequently, the Order evolved as a secret society in the north of Ireland and was extended to Upper Canada after 1815 with the immigration of Irish Protestants. Local lodges were formed and a grand lodge founded at Brockville in 1830. The goal of the Orange Order was 'the defence of Protestant Christianity and the unity of the Empire.'[6]

The Orange Lodge dominated Toronto throughout most of the 1800s and into the 1900s. Jesse Middleton wrote that it controlled the militia and municipal administration. From out of 80 mayors elected in Toronto, only 13 were not Orangemen, and, as late as 1923, only 4 of 29 aldermen were not members of the Lodge. Furthermore, through trustees and the inspectorate, the Orange Lodge controlled the public school system which fostered the training of pupils in its peculiar beliefs.[7] In December 1897, The *Catholic Register* commented upon the Orange domination:

of 767 positions in municipal employment, only 41 were held by Catholics; of the 255 positions on the police force, Catholics held 16; and in the jails and the courts, Catholics held none. Nor was there a single Catholic employee in City Hall itself:

> It is said the reason of this rigid exclusiveness is the existence in the City Hall of two co-operating lodges of the L.O.L. [Loyal Orange Lodge] and the S.O.E. [Sons of England] and that membership in one or other of these lodges is an indispensable condition of City Hall employment.[8]

The first Catholic hired at Toronto City Hall was Agnes Fay in the 1920s.

Irish were the majority offenders in the police courts and were frequently arrested for drunkenness and fighting by the Orange-controlled police force when others were not. Regardless of guilt or innocence, being Irish was often sufficient reason for conviction before an Orange judge. In order to escape the stigma and prejudice attached to being Irish, Irish Protestants abandoned the national designation and assimilated into the general Protestant society which was English and hostile to all things Irish. Even in the social institutions, those considered deserving poor were Protestants or hungry Irish Catholics turned craven for a bowl of soup.

But, as well, the Orange Order controlled the workplace, for most factory owners, managers, foremen, and lead hands were connected to it or to some allied society. In this realm the Irish Catholic worker had no protection. At the mercy of the lead hand, he was last hired and first fired. He had to take abuse about his nationality and religion and say little; to cause a riot in the workplace was irrational, for he could not win and would lose his employment.

The same type of differential treatment was applied to children. On one occasion, Irish Catholic children employed in a mill, knowing that the Protestant children had been allowed off on the twelfth of July to see the parade, asked permission to attend the annual separate school picnic. The request was denied with the statement "there are plenty of Mickeys to do the work". However, the children went to the picnic and the next day were refused admittance to the mill unless they forfeited a week's wages. They refused to work and were issued summonses under the Masters and Servants Act. *The Canadian Freeman* (Catholic) of August 1, 1887, ended its account of the incident with: "God help the Mickeys and their children."

The Brotherhood

In the middle decades of the 1800s, the Irish worker could rely upon the Irish Brotherhood, or 'the children', for some form of extra-legal protection. The Brotherhood had arisen from an amalgamation of the older societies common among the workers on the canals and operated from the Don flats and the shebeen shops (taverns). As a vigilante organization, it offered the Irish some collective protection from Orange abuse and retaliated against episodes of stone throwing, name calling, and more violent outbursts. Within its own ethnic community, the Brotherhood exercised some societal control by punishing Irishmen who beat their wives and children. But it was an anachronism in the organized, industrial setting. With the rise of a modern police force, the Irish worker lost some of his apprehension on the journey to work, as his children did on their journey to school. But once he entered the workplace, in most cases he was alone—the Mick, the Dogan, the Taig. By imposing isolation on him, Protestant workers did not realize that from it would evolve a counter-culture—for his mind was his own.

Unifying forces

Under the exertion of constant pressure to conform, the Irish Catholic community intensified its relationship with its Church, its only bulwark in the unfriendly city.

Concomitant with the expansion of the Church's metropolitan system, there was a growth of parish networks which included church, rectory, convent, schools, and hall with exclusive Irish Catholic organizations. And it was from within those parish networks that a counter-working-class culture developed and grew.

With its overriding emphasis on privatism, old societies like the St. Patrick Society, in which there had been considerable interaction with Irish Protestants, became obsolete. Many of the new ones were nationalistic but some, like the Hibernians, often caused cleavage within the community because of their sympathy with the Fenian movement.

For fear of jeopardizing the tenuous position of Irish Catholics in the city, the Church, with the consent of a number of its Irish adherents, denied the Hibernians the right to parade to the Cathedral in 1867. Within the group, religious sodalities and Irish Catholic benevolent associations flourished. The celebration of St. Patrick's Day, which had been the source of open conflict with the Orange Lodge, became more religiously oriented; Irish kin and friends gathered together for Mass, and parties afterwards.

In the early days, the shebeen society had been the centre of Irish culture. Friends and kin met to drink, sing, and fight, to discuss politics and to plan the strategy of the Irish community. But the Church disapproved of drinking, and its condemnation of it through sermons, literature, and temperance societies reduced participation in the shebeen society. Drinking continued as a facet of Irish culture but became more respectable by moving from the shebeen shops to public hotels. Catholic bookstores sold religious works and articles, Irish histories, and novels. Parish associations sponsored libraries to provide this literature to the working class. The Irish Catholic newspapers were central in the creation of an Irish Catholic identity, keeping the community informed of events and activities both local and abroad. They were replaced in the 1890s by Church-sponsored newspapers which retained an Irish outlook.

The separate schools in the city also perpetuated an Irish Catholic identity. In them, nuns and brothers of the same ethnic background taught academic subjects, religion, and Irish history, linking religion to nationalism and ethnicity. The pupils learned who they were, why they were here, and what their purpose in life must be, which instilled in them feelings of self-worth. Annual prize nights were well attended, giving the Irish community an opportunity to express pride in the accomplishments of its students and to enjoy a programme of Irish Catholic culture.

Bishop John Joseph Lynch.

In 1866 Bishop John Lynch recognized the elements which sustained Irish identity among his working class flock:

> *Irish history, Irish songs, Irish newspapers, Irish speeches at school, exhibitions, processions out on St. Patrick's Day to help keep up the Spirit of Irish Nationality in the country.*[9]

And as Irish Catholicism moved towards a working-class culture, the people and the Church retained certain elements of the cultural apparatus that had served them best in the past. Voluntary traits were utilized to create exclusive Irish Catholic religious, social, and secular organizations. Through organized voluntarism, which sponsored picnics, sporting events, bazaars, soirées, and lectures, the separate schools and social institutions were kept afloat. Irish Catholics from the hinterland were attracted to the larger events, while Irish workers from the urban centre mixed with members of the rural communities.

Sunday excursions to the shrine at Niagara not only gave the working-class a social outing but also fulfilled an age-old need from the Irish past. The belief in the curing powers of holy men, like Father McSpiritt, and in the Plaster of Knock imported from Ireland, became an important part of their culture, transposing the past practice in the old country pilgrimaging to holy wells for cures. Yearly missions brought men, women, and children to the Church to learn the precepts of their faith, to acquire role models for family life, to see the effects of their faults, and to realize the need to accept their situation with Christian forbearance. Failure to make the mission met with group censure, for it was considered a denial of faith and ethnicity. The community was cohesive; one did not join it, but was born into it. Marrying a Catholic who was not Irish was almost like marrying outside the faith.

The unity of the Irish community was strengthened by a belief in an Irish Catholic millennium. The group was commissioned to perform a historic task—the conversion of North America—and the improbability of it was never questioned. The beautification of church buildings and religious ceremonies, coupled with a system of devotional renewal, intensified an Irish sense of the Holy. Through it, the Irish working class found solace in the face of urban rejection, consolation in grief, and hope in the future. There was no class distinction in the act of worship. In the words of a Protestant observer at St. Michael's Cathedral:

> No difference was made on the score of dress or appearance; a very richly dressed lady and a poor old woman with faded calico dress and plain shawl occupied the same pew; the rough garb of the labouring man did not debar him from a good seat; a cluster of scantily clad little children was carefully looked after; and there was that cosmopolitan character about the congregation that seemed to fulfill the prayer of Him before whose cross they all bowed:—I pray that they may all be one.[10]

Fear of scorn, however, kept religion a private matter, for Protestants viewed Irish Catholics as a superstitious group, worthy of a derogatory stereotype. With the growing interaction between Church and people, priests became leaders in the community. Under their close supervision, many elements of discord were resolved.

With little distinction between the material and spiritual world, the Irish, in their fear of the dead, had held wild wakes. The drinking, fighting, and lewd games attached to them had been a source of embarrassment to the Church, and, through the influence of the priests and the St. Vincent de Paul Society, the wakes became more respectable, religious-oriented affairs. In a desire to maintain continuity with the deceased, the Irish had elaborate funerals and erected grand monuments, the costs of which were often beyond the means of this working-class population. To counteract this wasteful expense, the Church, through the Bona Mors Society, spread the concept that a good life was the only memorial needed. The Irish never lost the ability to laugh at themselves. Ethnic pride made them attempt to discourage the Victorian stereotype, epitomized by Irish comics in the music halls who brought laughter with "shure and bedad, who'll thread on the tail of me coat."[11]

Within the context of Irish Catholic culture, modesty became a virtue and family life was idealized. Earthly success was played down; failure was measured in terms of morality. In the workplace the distinctive culture was masked. There were few fights because the Church had taught the Irish to accept what happened with Christian forbearance. When work was done, the Irish workers left the workplace behind. They had little in common with Protestant workers because there was no intermarriage, no kin connections, nor any mutual organizations which they could join. Their voluntarism and organizational ability would later become an asset in the union movements. But they were to remain a separate entity because unions were mosaics, not melting pots.

References:

1. Gregory S. Kealey, "The Orange Order in Toronto: religious riot and the working class", in O'Driscoll and Reynold, *The untold story*, v.2, pp.829-851.

2. Murray Nicolson, "The Irish Catholics and social action in Toronto, 1850-1900", *Studies in History and Politics* ,v.1 (Sherbrooke: Bishops University, 1980).

3. *Journal of Education for Upper Canada* v.1(10), October 1848, p.300.

4. "A Protestant want", *Irish Canadian,* 21 June 1871.

5. *Irish Canadian*, 3 May 1856.

6. *Oxford Companion to Canadian History and Literature*, pp.616-617.

7. J. E. Middleton, *The municipality of Toronto: a history*, v.1 (Dominion Pub. Co., 1923), pp.786-798.

8. *The Catholic Register,* 23 December 1897.

9. Arcat, *Lynch papers,* Lynch to O'Donohue, 28 February 1866.

10. J. Ross Robertson, ed., *Robertson's Landmarks of Toronto:* a collection of historical sketches of the Old Town of York ... 4th ser. (Toronto, 1904), p.308.

11. *The Catholic Register,* 22 June 1893.

CHAPTER ELEVEN

SIX DAYS THOU SHALT LABOUR:

Joining the unions

Having equipped the Irish Catholics in Toronto with social institutions, the Church still had the dilemma of how to help its working class population in the industrial city. The bishops recognized that workers needed the protection of some formal organization to guarantee their right to earn a decent living. But in the 1850s and 1860s, most labour associations were secret, oath-bound societies based upon Masonic principles.

Freemasonry

For a number of reasons, Masonry has been condemned by every pope from Clement X in 1770 onwards. It is a secret society to which the Christian faith is incidental. In some European countries it has been extremely anti-clerical, indeed seeking the destruction of the Catholic Church. Catholics who joined the Masonic Order itself were excommunicated. In 1855, Bishop Armand de Charbonnel denied Irish Catholics who belonged to the Odd Fellows society their request to obtain permission to attend, as a body, religious services and funerals. In his Lenten Pastoral of 1859 Charbonnel defined his position clearly (and it applied to the Masons as well):

> That all the members of any society protecting its secrecy by an oath contrary to the prohibition of the church must be compelled under the penalty of the refusal of the sacraments, to retract that oath and give up the society, whatever may be laudable and of moderate and lawful defence.

Charbonnel's successor, Bishop John Joseph Lynch (1860-1888), recognized that this stand placed Irish

Catholic workers at a disadvantage. In 1872, he pointed out that they

> are excluded from the Church if they join secret Societies, and if they do not belong to the Free Masons, Odd Fellows or Orangemen they can scarcely receive a situation. The railroad companies are generally Masonic, the municipalities Orange, and the Government Employees are for the most part of both groups.[1]

From his earliest years as a priest, Lynch had been interested in the working man and his problems and now, with a bishop's authority, he began to conceive ways which would permit Catholic laymen to organize. Lynch must have been aware of the work of Bishop Von Ketteler of Mainz, Germany, who had called upon Catholics there to endow productive corporations for the workers and who stressed the value of craft organizations. When, in 1849, Karl Marx and Frederick Engels gave the world the *Communist Manifesto*, Bishop Von Ketteler was preaching on the rights of men and calling for state intervention on their behalf.

In his *Christianity and the Labour Question* (first published in English in 1864), Ketteler expressed the opinion that:

> it would be a great folly on our part if we kept aloof from this movement merely because it happens at the present time to be promoted chiefly by men who are hostile to Christianity. The air remains God's air though it be breathed by an atheist, and the bread we eat is no less the nourishment provided by God though kneaded by an unbeliever. It is the same with unionism: it is an idea which rests on the divine order of things, though the men who favour it do not recognize the finger of God in it, and often turn it to a wicked use.[2]

At first, Lynch attempted to limit the flow of unskilled Irish labourers to Toronto, perhaps thinking that their lot would not be improved in the new land where they would be discriminated against for their lack of manpower skills, their ethnicity, their religious beliefs, and their impoverished state. Concerned with the poor living standard of his labouring flock, he sent a circular to the bishops of Ireland in 1864 on "The Evils of Wholesale and Improvident Emigration From Ireland". Contrary to his instructions, the circular was widely published, and he was criticized by Church officials in Ireland and the United States for what they saw as a callous attitude. However, it is possible that his stand did not go unnoticed by various labour organizations. No doubt they could perceive that the bishop was primarily interested in the social conditions of the working man and not necessarily in increasing the number of Catholics in the city. Meanwhile, in 1870, Bishop Lynch became Archbishop, heading the new ecclesiastical province of Ontario bishops, separated from the Church province of Quebec for the first time.

Union organization

Throughout the 1870s and 80s, labour unrest was common and Toronto was penetrated by a number of union organizations claiming to be non-sectarian, without the requirement of secret oaths. Some, hoping to gain Church sanction so that Irish Catholics would be able to join, sent their proposals to Bishop Lynch for his approval or amendment. A particular request from the Iron Moulders International in 1873 asked Lynch to keep all correspondence confidential because the union did not want the public to know it was seeking Church sanction. In the same year, a group of locomotive engineers asked Lynch to support a petition to the Legislature. With the understanding that the society was neither secret nor illegal, Lynch agreed to sign it:

> ...to suppress, as far as possible, Sunday Traffic on Rail Roads, there appears to be no excuse for running freight trains, though there might be for running one passenger train, on Sundays: for instance to carry mails, or to assist

persons to attend the death bed of a friend or the like. In our modern civilization, no class of men is more deserving of our sympathy and respect than the Locomotive Engineers, and none deserve to be better remunerated for their service, for on their genius, sobriety, and care depend thousands of lives. Hence, in their well-being, we find safety for our own lives and property.[3]

But most unions and societies at that time did not represent the large element of unskilled Irish Catholic workers. However, the increased activity of Daniel O'Donoghue, a prominent Catholic labour figure, changed the picture. He had been a member of the Typographical Union and, in 1874, was elected to the Ontario Legislature as the first Labour candidate in Canada. With the revival of the American Knights of Labor in the 1880s, O'Donoghue became one of the leaders of this order in Toronto. This was an international, non-sectarian organization which enrolled skilled and unskilled workers, both men and women, and therefore appealed to the Irish Catholic working class.[4] And it was O'Donoghue and the Knights who swayed Lynch to the side of the worker against the growing antagonism of Cardinal Taschereau of Quebec City.

Knights of Labor

In 1883 Cardinal Emile Taschereau sent the Holy See a copy of the constitutions of the Knights of Labor, which was gaining support among French-Canadian workers. The Holy Office ruled that those who took part in the activities of the Order committed grave sin. As a result, the Cardinal condemned the Knights in his own diocese in 1884 and, as Primate of Canada, expected Lynch and the other bishops of Ontario to follow suit.

An appeal to Rome was supposed to have been invoked against the decision and, on that basis, Lynch and other bishops allowed Catholic workers to enroll or remain in the society. With the Holy See's subsequent silence,

Taschereau suspected that the appeal had not been sent and that Catholic workers had been deceived regarding the pronouncement of the Holy Office. For his part, Lynch, having received no direct communication from Rome, was not convinced of the Vatican directive. In March 1886, he

House of Providence, Toronto, c.1890.

confided to Rev. Dr. Funcken of Berlin (later Kitchener), Ontario, that the Knights of Labor and similar organizations had a well-known purpose— namely to negotiate better terms from employers for inadequately paid working men. Archbishop Lynch was convinced that the organization had no oath of secrecy, and that its objective was not to over-throw either the Church or the State. He reasoned that,

> *If we were to prevent our people from joining these working men societies , they should not get work, even in the United States, so that to prevent them from joining working men societies we must have certain proof of their being condemned by the Church, and each Bishop is not the Church.*[5]

In July 1886, after advising the Vatican of the difference of opinions expressed in Canadian and American newspapers concerning the Knights of Labor and the contention that the effect of Rome's sentence against it remained suspended by an appeal, Taschereau charged Lynch

> to proceed against that society according to the manner prescribed in the instruction of the 10th May, 1884. I do not see that at present there can be any doubt concerning the rule to be followed by Catholics of the whole world, over whom the jurisdiction of the Sacred Congregation extends.[6]

Meanwhile, Toronto industrialists were alarmed at the growing strength of the Knights of Labor. Among them was an Irish Catholic immigrant, Senator Frank Smith, who had amassed a fortune in wholesaling, banking, railways, and shipping, in addition to ownership of the Toronto Street Railway. Although he employed mostly Irish Catholics, they, like the other workers in the Toronto Street Railway, worked fourteen hours or longer, six days a week, for a weekly salary of $8.00 to $9.00.

One condition for employment included a pledge never to join any kind of labour organization. Each employee's conduct was governed by a strict set of rules, backed by fines or dismissal. When, in 1886, Smith dismissed three men for breach of this agreement, he only invigorated the need for organized labour in the view of his workers. Under the influence of Daniel O'Donoghue, Smith's Irish Catholic employees joined the Knights of Labor and became embroiled in a bitter strike. Although the strike failed, it had gained much support among workers who were generally dissatisfied with the service of the Street Railway System. Mocking Smith's complaint that his investments were damaged by the strike, a poem entitled "Senator Smith" was printed in The *Labour Reformer* of May 10, 1886:

> Behold the strangest sight e'er seen in all the lapse of years,
> A member of the Government, a Senator in tears.
> He says strikes are destroying him and scattering his wealth;
> And, worse than that, anxiety is breaking down

his health.
Oh, Smith, oh aged Senator, we hear your
plaintive cry,
But still the strike must on, old hoss, altho' you
fret and die,
And when you reach the place, old chap,
where bob-tailed
cars don't roll,
We pray the Lord have mercy on your bob-
tailed little soul.

Through the support of Lynch, Senator Frank Smith had gained political preferment by utilizing the threat of an Irish Catholic bloc vote. However, he alienated himself from his mentor, Archbishop Lynch, by defying him on separate school issues. Consequently, when the operation of the Toronto Street Railway was being disrupted it was left to Smith's wife to intercede. Knowing the influence the Archbishop had with Irish workers, Mrs. Smith appealed to him against labour during the strike. In a letter of July 1886, she accused the Knights of Labor of being masonic, secret, communist, anarchist, and socialist. She vilified its major promoter in Toronto, O'Donoghue, as a liar under the direction of an Orangeman, the Grand Master in Canada. The Knights, she said, were boycotting businesses to destroy them, thereby creating unemployment; and in their attempts to disrupt the Toronto Street Railway, they were resorting to violent action, including the use of dynamite. She called Cardinal Gibbons of the United States a sophist for supporting the Knights, and urged the Archbishop to uphold Cardinal Taschereau's condemnation of them. The workers, she said, had forgotten that their employer was also a labourer who worked harder than some of his men and could understand more than they —"one good head is worth a hundred pairs of hands at least."[7]

Lynch stands fast

For the opinions and problems of such "Lace Curtain" Irish, Archbishop Lynch had little sympathy. He was convinced that it would be wrong to support Taschereau's stand; to do so would deny the legitimate rights and demands of the Irish workers under his jurisdiction. And he remained firm in this position. A meeting of the Synod of Priests in Toronto on 16 September 1886 led to a cryptic memo to the clergy which read:

> Discussion was first opened informally regarding the Knights of Labor, especially on the effect of the alleged condemnation by Cardinal Taschereau. His Grace, Bishop O'Mahoney (Vicar General), and Archdeacon Cassidy participated—His Grace ended the discussion by declaring the order not condemned in this diocese.[8]

Meanwhile, a general condemnation against the Knights of Labor was being prepared in Rome, at the request of Cardinal Taschereau. Although the biographers, J. T. Ellis of Cardinal Gibbons of the United States, and J. Fitzsimmons of Cardinal Manning of Great Britain, credit these two cardinals as champions of the cause for the Knights of Labor, no doubt Archbishop Lynch's direction to the bishops of Ontario to defy the first Canadian Cardinal helped to bring the issue to a head. This was not accomplished without some feeling of trepidation on the part of Ontario's bishops, for it could be construed as ecclesiastical insubordination. They relied on Archbishop Lynch's sacred honour not to expose their opinions to Taschereau. Bishop J. Cleary of Kingston believed Taschereau had made a "curious mistake". In his opinion, "no disciplinary decision binds us, or the Ordinaries of any Province, unless it has been officially communicated to us by the Holy See. Rome has not thought fit to promulgate a decision concerning the Knights to us, and we are not bound to notice its delivery to Quebec."[9]

The English Cardinal Manning, who was to become famous for his support of the workers in the London dock strike of 1889, was convinced of the important role bishops played in their interaction with the laity. He advised the Holy Office that, "Up to the present the world has been governed by dynasties: henceforward the Holy See must treat with the people, and with bishops who are in close daily and personal relations with the people."[10]

Holding the same view on the Knights of Labor as Archbishop Lynch, Cardinal Gibbons of Baltimore, after consultation with Manning, decided to go to Rome as a spokesman for the American bishops. Lynch was kept informed of the planning stages by his friend Henry O'Brien, who travelled extensively in the United States and had the ear of many prominent members of the Curia. On 19 September 1886, O'Brien advised Lynch from Baltimore that the American bishops were of the opinion that no harsh measures would be adopted because "the organization is so powerful that it must be guided or the Church will lose its backbone." And from Rome on January 22, 1887, he expressed the opinion that, when Gibbons arrived, "the question of the Knights of Labor will be settled—certainly favourably." Concerning another issue, he stated that it, "like the decree against the Knights of Labor,...will be a dead letter."[11]

On 20 February 1887, Cardinal Gibbons presented a strong case on behalf of the Knights of Labor to Cardinal Simeoni, Prefect of the Sacred Congregation of the Propaganda, the context of which was reprinted in Toronto in *The Catholic Weekly Review,* March 10, 1887. In his argument, Gibbons affirmed that the organization was neither masonic nor hostile to the Church, and was essential because monopolies controlled legislation. He stated that workers—men, women and children—had a right to protect themselves, and that failure to recognize this in a democratic country was a dangerous step. Condemnation of that group would only open the doors to other groups. As well, if the Knights was censured, the Holy See would lose its working members' contributions to Peter's Pence, and the support of the Universal Church would be undermined, as would the authority of the bishop.

Concurrently, Lynch wrote Cardinal Gibbons with satisfaction and "expectations of self-esteem" because he "had already taken" His Eminence's "views on the same question." In this letter, Lynch described how and why he had arrived at the conclusion which compelled him to defy his ecclesiastical superior. He had "had interviews with the chief officers in Canada of the Knights of Labor who were good conscientious Catholics." Having examined their constitutions, their private bills and by-laws, he found nothing contrary to the Church or to the well-being of society. Instead, he believed the Knights was constituted to prevent a revolution similar to what occurred in France — "the poor against the monopoly and oppressions of the rich." He saw that Ontario was under the power of a "combination of capitalistic corporations"— in mines, railroads, manufacturing — wherein the working men "who gained immense riches for those companies were kept on starving wages, not enough in the majority of cases to supply the natural wants of their families." Because "capital was organized for its own purposes in wealth," Lynch believed "working men must then organize in self-defence, that they would gain by the sweat of their brow enough to enable them to work and to support their families." That arrangement, in Lynch's mind, would benefit both groups; it would secure the position of the labourer and allow the capitalists to accumulate money for future use.

Lynch also expressed deep concern about the growing secularization in Toronto. In the rapidly expanding urban population, where needs had to be quickly met, "religion is kept in the background ... very little spoken of amongst working men." However, it seems he was confident in the private faith of his own flock, for he observed that "the majority of the Knights of Labor are Irish men well grounded in their faith by persecution, obedient to the Church in a most remarkable degree." Knowing that his Irish Catholics had "to join some union," he was pleased that, "in preference to others," the Knights of Labor was "free from objectionable features." However, he correctly surmised that the "society was not of a permanent nature," believing that it arose "for a certain lawful purpose to remedy an evil," which Lynch mistakenly thought would be "shortly cured" when capitalism realized "the necessity of work as the advantage of fair dealing with the working men."

Regarding his defiance of Taschereau, Lynch expressed sadness for the workers in the Province of Quebec, deprived of the sacraments of the Church because their "spiritual guides are misinformed or all too apprehensive of an imaginary evil that the rules of the Knights of Labor may bring on." If he had supported Taschereau's stand, Lynch believed he would have placed a barrier between the Church and the working class.[12]

Bishop John Walsh.

Bishop John Walsh of London—like Lynch, born in Ireland—who was soon to succeed Lynch as Archbishop of Toronto, commended the latter for the manner in which he had dealt with the labour question. He believed Lynch's approach was "simple, clear and convincing" and if "widely circulated it could not fail to do a great deal of good."[13] When the Holy Office ultimately ruled in favour of the Knights of Labor, Lynch wrote Taschereau, explaining that he upheld the Knights of Labor to assure continued religious practice in the Irish working class.[14]

Rerum novarum

It was the preliminary work of these bishops and others in Europe which prompted the Church to define the rights and responsibilities of the labourer. On 15 May 1891, Pope Leo XIII issued the papal encyclical, *Rerum novarum,* On the conditions of labour. In it, the Pope elevated the position of the common working man, saying, "God himself chose to seem and to be considered the son of a carpenter—nay, did not disdain to spend a great deal of His life as a carpenter Himself."

Archbishop Walsh, Lynch's successor, released the English translation of the document, and commentaries on it were printed in the *Catholic Weekly Review*. These stated clearly that the labourer's skill was the capital he invested and that therefore he should share in the profit. In addition to the right to receive an adequate return for his labour, the worker had the responsibility to keep the law—for it safeguarded his own freedom—to strike only as a drastic measure against injustice, and to promote arbitration between capital and labour.

Other labour issues

Regardless of unions, workers remained divided over other issues. The Sunday Streetcar question of 1893 was an example. Catholics wanted streetcars to run on Sunday to accommodate recreation. Archbishop Walsh was in agreement, reasoning that, after attending Mass, workers in their free time should have some means to get to the outskirts of the city for some fresh air. However, Protestant churches, the Orange Order, and the Sons of Ireland Protestant Association, afraid of the implications of an open Sunday in the European style, were averse to the operation of streetcars on the Sabbath. So the Knights of Labor joined the 22,000 Irish Catholics who favoured the proposal, while Daniel O'Donoghue and other union leaders placed themselves in the Sabbatarian camp because they feared that operation of Sunday streetcars could be utilized to extend the work week. Quite clearly, as late as 1893, religion and ethnicity played conflicting roles in the working man's world.

The Church never came to terms with socialism because of the revolutionary and anti-religious attitude of its proponents. However, through its newspaper, *The Catholic Register*, it pressed for the rights of working men, and, when they were unemployed, as in the depression of the

1890s, attacked the city of Toronto for its inequity, bias, and callousness.

Rights of working women

Although advocating the principal role of women as wives and mothers, the Church also recognized that women were entering the working world in ever-increasing numbers. Their rights, too, needed to be protected. Hence, Archbishop Walsh endorsed the Women's Protective Association. Father F. Ryan was appointed Walsh's spokesman to that group and, in addressing it, he made it clear that

> I am here representing the Catholic Church, the Church of the people, and that Church will assist in every way to ameliorate the suffering of and protect the working women, and that to this movement the Church as well as I add its blessing.[15]

Conclusion

The Catholic Church in Victorian Toronto, being Irish in head and members, found it natural to assist the Irish Catholic working-class. Recognizing the injustice of industrial capitalism, the Church supported unions once they were cleared from secret oaths to a hostile ideology.

References:

1. Arcat, *Lynch papers*, Lynch to Frank Smith, 1 February 1872.
2. Bishop Von Kettler, *Christianity and the labour question*, cited in N. McKenna, "Catholics and labor unions", B. L. Masse, ed., *The Catholic mind through fifty years ,1903 to 1953* (New York: American Press, 1953), p.563.
3. *Op cit.*, Lynch to R. Pearson, 29 April 1873.
4. J. G. O'Donoghue, *Daniel John O'Donoghue, Father of the Canadian labour movement* (Toronto: Canadian Catholic Historical Association, 1942), pp.87-96.
5. Archives of the Congregation of the Resurrection, Lynch to Rev. Dr. Funcken, 31 March 1886.
6. Arcat, *Lynch papers*, from Taschereau, Memo to My Lord, 31 July 1886.
7. *Ibid.*, Mrs. F. Smith to Lynch, 5 July 1886.

8. *Ibid.*, memo to clergy, 16 September 1886.

9. *Ibid.*, Bishop Cleary to Lynch, undated.

10. J. Fitzsimmons, "Manning and the workers", J. Fitzsimmons, ed., *Manning: Anglican and Catholic* (London, 1951), p.142.

11. Arcat, *Lynch papers*, H. O'Brien to Archbishop Lynch, 19 September 1886.

12. *Ibid.*, Lynch to Cardinal Gibbons, 23 March 1887.

13. *Ibid.*, Walsh to Archbishop Lynch, 30 March 1887.

14. *Ibid.*, Lynch to Cardinal Taschereau, 23 April 1887.

15. *The Catholic Register,* 18 June 1893.

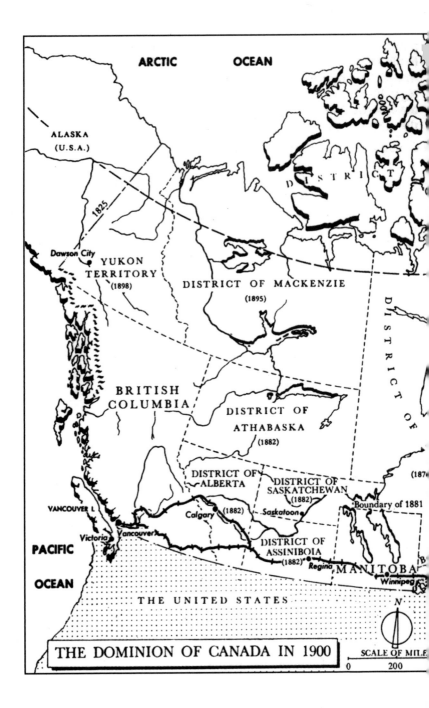

ARCTIC OCEAN

ALASKA
(U.S.A.)

D I S T R I C T

1825

Dawson City

YUKON
TERRITORY
(1898)

DISTRICT OF MACKENZIE
(1895)

D
I
S
T
R
I
C
T

O
F

BRITISH
COLUMBIA

DISTRICT OF
ATHABASKA
(1882)

DISTRICT OF
ALBERTA

DISTRICT OF
SASKATCHEWAN
(1882)

(187

VANCOUVER I.

Calgary   (1882)

Saskatoon

Boundary of 1881

Victoria   Vancouver

PACIFIC

DISTRICT OF
ASSINIBOIA
(1882)   Regina   MANITOBA   B

OCEAN

Winnipeg

THE UNITED STATES

N

THE DOMINION OF CANADA IN 1900

SCALE OF MILE

0   200

136

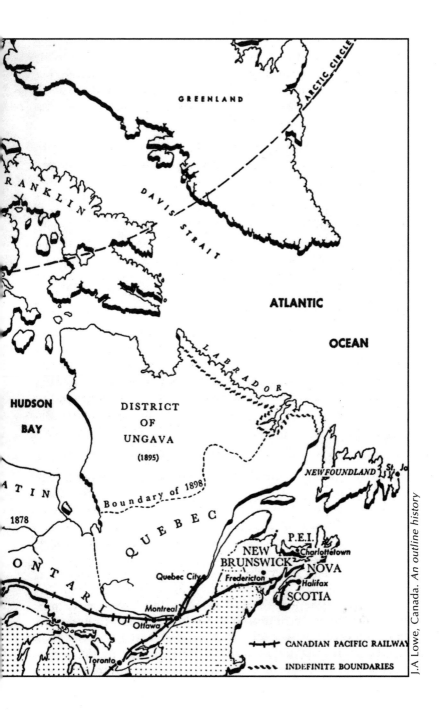

GREENLAND

ARCTIC CIRCLE

RANKLIN

DAVIS STRAIT

ATLANTIC

OCEAN

LABRADOR

HUDSON

BAY

DISTRICT
OF
UNGAVA
(1895)

NEWFOUNDLAND   St. Jo

Boundary of 1898

ATIN

1878

P.E.I.
Charlottetown

QUEBEC

NEW
BRUNSWICK

NOVA
SCOTIA

ONTARIO

Quebec City   Fredericton

Halifax

Montreal

Ottawa

Toronto

+—+—+ CANADIAN PACIFIC RAILWAY

^^^^ INDEFINITE BOUNDARIES

J.A Lowe, Canada. *An outline history*

137

CHAPTER TWELVE

FROM IRISH STOCK
TO MANY NATIONS

As the 19th century was drawing to a close, Canada had begun to play a minor role on the world scene. The completion of the railway coast-to-coast had opened the doors to a wealth of natural resources and provided access to employment opportunities across the land. Mining, logging, industry, farming, city-building—all needed labourers and settlers. And yet, more people were leaving the country than entering it. In addition, for the first time since Confederation, volunteer troops were being sent abroad to assist the British against the Boer forces in South Africa, laying bare the French/English issue of imperialism versus nationalism.

What Canada needed at that period of history was a workforce. And what threatened the basic future of English Protestant Canadian society was the influx of a 'foreign' element. On the whole, Irish Catholics, aside from their religious affiliation, by that time identified with the broader English-speaking population.

Laurier and immigration

In response to business and railway interests, and with the development of an agricultural market and the demand for hard wheat, Wilfrid Laurier's government, elected in 1896, implemented a program of large-scale immigration that intensified from 1903 to 1913. Clifford Sifton, the federal Minister of the Interior, in seeking to people the West, was willing to allow entry to those from places other than the British Isles, Northern Europe, and the United States. He admitted: "A stalwart peasant in a sheepskin coat, born on the soil, whose forefathers have been farmers for ten generations, and a stout wife and a half-dozen children is good quality."[1]

That statement, however, did not mirror prevailing public opinion or Canadian immigration policies, which were unabashedly racist. Sifton and his immigration authorities listed preferred settlers in a descending order, barely opening the door to those in "sheepskin coats." At the top were British and American agriculturalists, followed by French, Belgians, Dutch, Scandinavians, Swiss, Finns, Russians, Austro-Hungarians, Germans, Ukrainians, and Poles. Next came those believed less assimilable: Italians, South Slavs, Greeks, and Syrians. Asians, Jews, Gypsies, and Blacks were at the bottom because, according to a newspaper account, like the Italians, "they don't farm well."[2]

What was the impact of that "foreign" contingent on the English-speaking Catholic population, particularly in Ontario? While the government sought commitments to obtain agricultural and resource labourers for isolated areas, many of the immigrants, non-English- speaking and non-Protestant, did not comply. They chose instead to work in the cities like Toronto and Hamilton, rekindling the ethno-religious prejudices previously directed towards the Irish. In fact, in a 1897 series of articles entitled "Foreigners who live in Toronto" written for the *Daily Mail and Empire*, a Toronto newspaper, the future Prime Minister Mackenzie King described the Irish, Scots, English, Americans, and Newfoundlanders as "nearly akin in thought, customs and manners to the Canadians themselves," thus excluding them from the definition. It seems that religious tensions between Irish Catholics and other British immigrants were insignificant in view of a common language. Those who stood out in King's discussions were Germans, Jews, Italians, Syrians, and, remarkably, French Canadians.[3]

French Canadians

The French Canadians accounted for 800 of Toronto's

population, and were mainly employed in factories. Being linguistically isolated within the English-speaking city, they desired to continue religious practice in their own language. Consequently, the Archbishop of Toronto requested the Archbishop of Montreal to send a priest to serve their needs, which was the foundation of Paroisse Sacré-Coeur in 1887. The children of these French parishioners attended the separate schools and most spoke English well.[4] But linguistic hostility was sparked in other parts of the province when, in 1910, Bishop Michael Fallon of the London diocese led Irish Catholic opposition to bilingual schools. His intervention would have far-reaching effects on both provincial and federal politics.

With the influx of French speakers into the Ottawa Valley, many separate schools gave instruction in French, offering English as just another curriculum subject. Taking a stand against this practice, the Ontario Conservative government issued Regulation 17 in 1912 which limited the use of French in the classroom to the first two years. Franco-Ontarians were outraged. The conflict flared again in 1915 when the Ottawa Separate School Board, predominantly French, refused to comply with the Regulation or to discipline teachers who continued to teach in the French language. The government was supported by English-speaking Catholics who, as instigated by Bishop Fallon, endeavoured to keep the French "in their place". In February of 1916, 122 French teachers in Ottawa went on strike, leaving 4,000 French children without instruction. The teachers had been unpaid because the city withheld $83,000 in separate school taxes.

In November of the same year, the Judicial Committee of the British Privy Council ruled that the Ontario government had the right to decide the language taught in provincial schools. That decision had repercussions for Wilfrid Laurier's federal Liberal party which, in 1917, split along French-English linguistic lines. Compulsory military duty, known as conscription, was proposed by Tory Prime

Minister Robert Borden, to compensate for the decline in volunteers to the World War I offensive. The proposal, while resented by Ontario and prairie farmers and by various ethnic communities, was most strongly opposed in Quebec, still smarting from the anti-French-language school policies in Ontario. Gaining the support of pro-conscription Liberals in Ontario, the Tory government was swept back into power, leaving Laurier with 82 Liberal seats—mostly in Quebec.[5]

Germans

Until the advent of World War I, the Germans, next to the British, enjoyed a preferred immigrant status and, at the time of Confederation, formed the largest of the foreign groups. Viewed as hard-working and conservative, they posed no threat because they were dispersed and isolated. The Catholics among them settled in Perth, Huron, Bruce, and Grey counties in Ontario. Some resided in Toronto where the majority of Germans were Protestant. As early as 1881, a few German services for the Catholics of the community were held at St. Patrick's Church on McCaul Street, built for Toronto's Irish Catholics in 1861.

The largest German settlement in Ontario was in Waterloo County, with Berlin as its urban centre. The combination of agriculture and industry provided the area with a booming economy. Its Catholic population was guided by the Congregation of the Resurrection, whose priests, Eugene Funkin, Louis Funkin, Theobald Spetz, and John Fehrenbach, established St. Jerome's College, where German was taught, although all courses were conducted in English. Intense nationalism during the war of 1914-1918 fostered an anti-German sentiment that forced the citizens of Berlin to change its name to Kitchener in 1916. Across the country, previously respected Germans were now labelled "enemy aliens". Some were dismissed from their jobs and some were placed in internment camps. The use of their mother language was either restricted or banned.

Syrians

Mackenzie King, in an 1897 article, commented on the presence of Syrians in Toronto, about 50 or 60 of them, who "have also in their midst a Catholic Syrian priest." The reference was to Father Macarios Nasr, a Melkite, who was allowed to conduct services at St. Patrick's Church. After six months, however, Nasr had to find another church because "our presence is very expensive."

The St. Vincent de Paul Society offered its hall on Shuter Street and it became the religious centre for Syrians, mostly Melkites and some Maronites, who were engaged as confectioners, importers, peddlers, and rug repairmen. When the hall was sold in 1911, the Syrian community appealed to the Latin-rite Catholic diocese for help. The Syrians were granted permission to use the basement of St. Michael's Cathedral for services and to start a Church Building Fund.

By 1913, however, the Syrian community was being torn apart by theological conflicts between adherents of the Maronite and Melkite Rites and by arguments about Syrian versus Lebanese identity. The Melkites created Our Lady of Assumption parish and the Maronites worshipped at Our Lady of Mt. Carmel. Both communities maintained separate religious and ethnocultural identities, but English was the language of their children at school. In 1922, the pastor left the Maronite for the Latin Rite and "their community atrophied".

Much more threatening than the small number of Syrians were the Poles, Ukrainians, and Italians, whose cultures, in the eyes of the Protestant majority, were morally inferior and whose religion was steeped in superstition. It was feared that their lifestyles would disrupt the social fabric of the country. While the Catholic hierarchy sought to retain religious affiliation by establishing national parishes, the Protestant clergy, chiefly the Methodists and Presbyterians, strove to assimilate them by upholding the social gospel to improve their lot. This contest for souls was not merely confined to Protestant versus Catholic in Ontario, but became a struggle between English and French for domination in Western Canada.

Polish immigrants

The first homogeneous group of Poles emigrated from German-held territory (Poland was not a nation-state until 1918) and settled in Renfrew County, Ontario, in 1858. The second wave of immigration (1895-1913) included family groups, many of whom received land grants and set up farms in Manitoba and the western prairies. However, in that period some of them, mostly "single men, or men with families left behind," were attracted to the employment opportunities and wages offered in the cities of Ontario.

Meanwhile Toronto, with its booming economy, attracted rural Canadian youths who left school to seek jobs. As a result, there was in 1901 a housing crisis; low-rent housing in the $8 to $25 range was almost impossible to find. Thus the Polish men, mostly unskilled, struggled to survive in the immigrant ward with its slum conditions. Drawn together by their language and religion, a group of them met in 1905 at St. Patrick's Church "to recite the Rosary in Polish and the Little Hours to the Virgin Mary."

That meeting precipitated the formation of St. Stanislaus Parish. Through the missionary efforts of the Congregation of the Resurrection in Waterloo, a priest visited to hold services in Polish at three of Toronto's downtown churches: St. Michael's Cathedral, St. Patrick's, and St. Mary's Church on Bathurst Street. These were attended by a number of Slavonic people. Concerned with their plight, particularly that of the young Polish men, with no English, unskilled and illiterate, the priest in 1907 alerted Toronto's Archbishop Dennis O'Connor to the need for a permanent clergyman to guide them. In 1911, Irish Catholic brewer Eugene O'Keefe purchased a former Presbyterian church for the Polish congregation, who, under Rev. Jóseph Hinzman, established St. Stanislaus Parish in the heart of what was to become a Polish neighbourhood. Four years later, St. Mary's also became a Polish parish.

While the Polish Catholics organized to develop mutual benefit societies to provide financial assistance to those in need, they also were "involved in preserving national culture and Polish identity." But the outbreak of the World War in 1914 had a tremendous impact on Polish communities in Canada. Citizens' committees were organized to gather financial contributions to help the Polish army in France, and to convince Canadian authorities that Polish immigrants from German-held territories should not be interned as enemy aliens. Recruitment centres were set up, an unofficial one at St. Stanislaus' Church, to obtain volunteers to join their compatriots in France. These North American efforts were said to have been "decisive in the formation of a free Polish republic after World War One." What they also did was solidify Polish associations and culture. Having depended on their own resources, many Polish Catholics, reflecting a North American view of their role, wanted more responsibility in the operation of their parishes. In some cases this led to defection from the Roman Catholic Church to the Polish National Catholic Church.[6]

Ukrainians

Most Ukrainian immigrants settled in Western Canada. Some were Orthodox, some known as latynnyky attached to the Roman Latin Rite, but the majority were Byzantine Greek Catholics, following the tradition of the Eastern rite, but recognizing the authority of the pope. Within the Ukrainian Byzantine Catholic rite there were many married priests.

A contentious issue stemmed from the Vatican's decision in 1894, at the prompting of the American hierarchy, to prohibit married clergy from serving in North America.

This left a vacuum that Latin-rite Catholic clergy scarcely penetrated. Hoping to solve the problem, the Canadian hierarchy laid the foundation, in 1910, to establish a Ukrainian bishopric for Canada in Winnipeg. Included in the plans were financial aid, clerical support, and the preparation of Ukrainian candidates for the priesthood at St. Augustine's Seminary in Toronto.

In 1912, Nykyta Budka was appointed Ukrainian bishop for all of Canada. The fact that Budka was reliant on French clergy and English money only heightened the suspicions of some Ukrainians opposed to what they saw as centralization and latinization of their Church. Consequently some abandoned the Ukrainian rite to join the Orthodox church. (Note: Bishop Budka eventually returned to Ukraine where he suffered martyrdom in 1945-46 together with all other Ukrainian and Greek Catholic bishops there, when Stalin forcibly dissolved the Eastern Rite Catholic Church, arresting tens of thousands of laity and priests, and expropriating their several thousand churches and properties, to be given to the Orthodox church.)

A few Ukrainian immigrants, mostly young single men, arrived in the cities of Ontario, often by way of the United States. An article in Toronto's *People* describes the experience of three of the first arrivals in 1903. They were overheard on the street, speaking their language, by a Galician Jew delivering bread. He brought them to his bakery on York Street, fed them, and arranged accommodation at a friend's boarding house. The next day, the Jewish landlord took them to the Canadian Pacific Railway Company where they got jobs laying sewer pipes at fifteen cents an hour.

The goal of the young immigrants to the cities was to earn money to buy land on the Prairies or to return to Ukraine to farm. Always in search of higher-paying jobs, their lifestyle was transient. They were excellent workers and took on difficult, distasteful and dangerous labouring work. In Toronto, they lived in the centre of the city in St.

John's ward which extended from the railway to just north of the old city hall, and which was the primary immigrant receiving area. Some lived in Jewish boarding houses where a common language dispelled the loneliness.

By 1911, there were 2,500 Ukrainians in Toronto alone. The latynnyky joined in services with the Poles and, in fact, made up a good proportion of the laity at St. Stanislaus Parish when it opened. The Ukrainian Catholics waited for a priest of their own and from 1909 to 1911 were attended occasionally by a visiting priest from Buffalo. Mass was celebrated in a private home in West Toronto Junction, which became an area of Ukrainian concentration located close to newly opened plants. In 1911 the Ukrainians were given the use of St. Helen's Church, built for the Irish in 1875. Bishop Budka stopped in Toronto on his way to Winnipeg, and on December 12, 1912, celebrated his first Mass on Canadian soil at St. Helen's. By 1914, the Ukrainian Catholic community in Toronto worked together to build its own church, St. Josaphat's, which became a focal point of religious and cultural life.

At the outbreak of the War, Toronto was the largest Ukrainian centre in Eastern Canada. Under the War Aliens Act, most Ukrainian immigrants had to register and report regularly to the police station. In many ways this helped to stabilize the Ukrainian community. As for these 'enemy aliens', they managed to volunteer 10,000 troops to serve in the Canadian army.

Italians

In the first wave of Italian immigration (1900 to 1914), 119,700 Italians entered Canada, primarily through the United States, and settled in the major urban centres of Ontario. Eighty percent were young men, labourers who worked in the mines and bush of Northern Ontario, in seasonal construction work, and in factories, returning to the city during winter months. They took advantage of educational opportunities offered by the Frontier College to "bunkhouse" men, and signed up for English classes at the non-sectarian Central Neighbourhood in the Ward and at the Little Flower Methodist Mission in the heart of what was known in Toronto as Little Italy. Struggling to survive, they wanted to speak English to cope in the new environment and were not concerned about being "brought back to Jesus."

Besides the young labourers, Italians were employed as barbers, tailors, peddlers, bakers, shoemakers, street musicians, and fruit vendors. Some who began as fruit vendors became grocers and provisioners. Families grew and children became proficient in English and prospered. The Archdiocese of Toronto established an Italian parish in 1908, Our Lady of Mount Carmel. Mutual aid societies were established and newspapers founded and, most importantly, the value of the extended family as a social institution flourished, regardless of how outsiders saw them. At the beginning of the War, Italian immigrants were viewed with suspicion, and discrimination against them resulted in increased unemployment. The picture changed, however, when Italy joined Britain in the war effort in 1915. Italy's emigration legislation had a clause that had an impact on reservists in time of war. Thus, Italian immigrants were hailed as heroes as they travelled through Canadian cities to join the fight abroad. However, their families, in many cases having lost the breadwinner, were forced to rely on public charity.

Protestant frowning

In June of 1913, at the Presbyterian Church's General Assembly in Toronto, ministers involved in Canadian missionary work urged the curbing of immigration. Complaining about their illiteracy, their pauperism, their fondness for liquor, Rev. W. D. Reid added that immigrants "are also bringing in and propagating socialist doctrines." According to Rev. S. W. Kinsdale:

> *Responsibility rests with Anglo-Saxons for allowing immigrants to continue in patterns set in foreign, mainly Roman Catholic countries.... Protestant churches must keep immigrants from falling into 'the clutches of the rum-seller, the Jewish usurer, and the slave-driver.*[7]

The Great War interrupted the immigration process. The spread of the Spanish Flu at its conclusion had a devastating and far-reaching effect. Added to that, the political and economic upheaval in Europe forced Canada to re-examine its immigration policies.

By the 1920s the Irish were a part of the English majority, while the Catholic Church, in its attempts to serve its faithful of different tongues, had promoted a multicultural society that would continue to flourish with the changing patterns of future immigration.

References:

1. Harold Troper, "Immigration", *The Canadian Encyclopedia* (Edmonton: Hurtig Pub., 1988), p.1046.

2. "Sifton unveils plans for biggest immigration push of the century", *Chronicle of Canada* (Montreal: Chronicle Pubs., 1990), p.472.

3. Robert E. Harney, ed., *Polyphony and Toronto's people* (Multicultural History Society of Ontario, 1984), v.6(1), p.1.

4. "Foreigners who live in Toronto", *The Daily Mail and Empire,* 2 October 1897.

5. See, in general, Robert Choquette, *Language and religion: a history of English-French conflict in Ontario* (Ottawa: University of Ottawa Press, 1975).

6. Zofia Shahrodi, "The experience of Polish Catholics in the Archdiocese of Toronto", in M. G. McGowan and B. P. Clarke, eds., *Catholics at the "gathering place"* (Toronto: Canadian Catholic Historical Society, 1993), pp.141-154.

7. "Curb immigration, missionaries urge", *The Chronicle of Canada,* p. 554.

Book Index

Elmsley, John 43, 58, 63, 74, 75, 80, 82

Fallon, Michael O.M.I., Bishop of London (1909-1931) 140
Family Compact 46
Fehrenbach, Father John 141
Fleming, Michael, Bishop of St. John's, NF (1830-1850)
  24, 25
Fraser, William, Bishop of Antigonish, NS (1844-1851) 37
Freemasons 122
Funcken, Father F. 126
Funkin, Father Eugene 141
Funkin, Father Louis 141

Gaulin, Remi, Bishop of Kingston, ON (1840-1849) 31, 50, 53
Gibbons, Edward, Cardinal, Archbishop of Baltimore, USA
  128, 129, 130, 131
Globe 79, 113
Grandin, Vital O.M.I., Bishop of Edmonton, AB (1871-
  1902) 89, 93, 95, 97, 99
Grant, Cuthbert 92
Grey Nuns 69, 70, 90, 91, 93

Italians 139, 142, 146, 147

Jesuits (Society of Jesus) 12, 61, 69, 85
Jubilee Riots (1875) 107, 108

King, MacKenzie 139, 142
Knights of Labor 125, 127, 129, 130 131, 132, 133

Lacombe, Father Albert O.M.I. 94, 95
La Flèche, Father Louis, 93
Langevin, Adelard, O.M.I., Archbishop of St, Boniface
  (1895 1915) 103, 105
Laurier, Wilfrid, Prime Minister 105, 140
Laval, François de Montmorency, Bishop of Quebec (1658-
  1687) 14
Leo XIII, Pope (1873-1903) 132
Loretto Sisters (IBVM) 61, 79
Lynch, John Joseph, Bishop & Archbishop of Toronto

151